REVIEWS FOR *ENGAGING ISLAM*

"Few persons have so faithfully 'laid down their lives' that Muslims might find the Lord Christ and eternal life as Georges Houssney. I've watched his life and ministry since 1968...he's earned the right to exhort and teach us all."

Dr. Greg Livingstone
Founder of Frontiers

"I have had the privilege of personal friendship with Georges Houssney for over forty years. He is one who walks the talk, which is why I am so excited about this strategic, must-read book. I will be getting one hundred copies ASAP to give to friends, especially pastors and leaders. Being born in Lebanon and growing up and serving in that part of the world gives him insight that many writers about Islam will not have."

Dr. George Verwer
Founder of Operation Mobilization, author, renowned speaker, world missions advocate

"The transformation of Georges Houssney, from a teenage hater of Muslims to a rest-of-his-life lover of Muslims, is a story of God's overcoming grace. In this book you will find down-to-earth, practical examples of not only loving Muslims, but seeing them come to Christ, both here in the States and in several countries around the world. The case studies are invaluable for all who would like to work with their Muslim neighbors. And along the way, Houssney gives a very balanced and realistic picture of what Islam really teaches. The title should be "Engaging Muslims," for that is what the author has done his entire adult life and up to this present time. If the average evangelical would read and follow the teaching in this book, we would see a change in the political and religious landscape of our land."

Dr. Don McCurry, President, Ministries to Muslims
Author of *Healing the Broken Family of Abraham*

REVIEWS FOR *ENGAGING ISLAM*

"With a magic smile and shining eyes, Georges Houssney welcomes students, international visitors, church people, and mosque people, switching from English to Arabic with no trouble at all. Beneath Boulder's blue sky, and across the street from the University of Colorado, Houssney runs a dorm for international students. There, they discover what it means to be cared for.

"But beyond the pine forests of the Rocky Mountains, Houssney has a heart for his homeland, Lebanon, and for Arabs everywhere. In his Engaging Islam courses, he trains people to befriend Muslims. In other camps and conferences, he helps followers of Jesus from Muslim backgrounds to connect and take courage from one another. Academic courses are fine, but witness can lead to agony, tough choices can result, and cutting-edge guidance may be hard to find.

"Houssney stands in the gap, wrestling with the academic as well as the practical and real human dilemmas of following Jesus. Georges empowers others to serve in the name of Jesus."

    Miriam Adeney, Ph.D., Associate Professor of Global and Urban Ministry, Seattle Pacific University; Teaching Fellow, Regent College; Adjunct Professor, Fuller Theological Seminary
    Author of *Daughters of Islam* and *Kingdom Without Borders: The Untold Story of Global Christianity*

"I am so glad Georges has put decades of personal experience and creative communication skills into the writing of this book. The resultant, well-documented, well-argued text comes across as a writing of the heart–and Georges has a large heart! I hope that readers will be informed by a competent commentator on Islam and challenged by a man with a holy passion to share the Gospel with Muslim friends."

    Rt. Rev. Dr. Bill Musk, Assistant Bishop for North Africa and Rector of St. George's Church in Tunisia
    Author of *The Unseen Face of Islam* and several other books on Islam

REVIEWS FOR *ENGAGING ISLAM*

"Reading Georges Houssney's book, Engaging Islam, was like being taken on a guided tour into the world of Islam, and shown firsthand how to engage Muslims with the transforming power of the Gospel. One soon realizes that Georges is not leading us on some academic exercise, but rather on a journey that sums up his heart's passion and his life's work, which has been to reach Muslims for Christ. It does not take long to realize the privilege the reader has to learn from a man who has ministered among Muslims for over forty years. His wealth of experience ministering among Muslims and training others to do so provides him with plenty of personal experience to draw from. His lifetime of study provides him with penetrating insights into the mind and heart of Muslims, which will be an invaluable resource for all who have been called into ministering among Muslims. His practical instructions on how to engage Muslims should be studied by every missionary candidate to the Muslim world. His confidence in the power of the cross to transform the Muslim who comes to faith in Jesus Christ will inspire every reader to want to get started in engaging his Muslim neighbors for Christ."

Rev. Tat Stewart, Talim Ministries, Minister at Large to the Persian speaking world, teaching and mentoring Persian speaking leaders

"Engaging Islam, by Georges Houssney, is an outstanding work about how Christians can be effective in engaging Muslims and reaching them with the Gospel. Georges comes from a Middle East Christian background in Lebanon, so he writes from personal experience in engaging Muslims. His book displays a broad knowledge of Islam and Arab culture, and recounts many stories of Muslims who have come to Christ. I have known Georges and his work for years and can recommend him and his book."

Rev. Sam Schlorff, Th.M. missiologist, veteran Arab World Ministries missionary
Author of *Missiological Models in Ministry to Muslims*

Engaging
Islam

Georges Houssney

Engaging Islam by Georges Houssney

Editors: Pierre Houssney, and
Greg Smith, Black Lake Studio, LLC (blacklakestudio.com)

Cover Design: Zef Houssney
Cover Art: André Houssney

This is a work of nonfiction. In some cases, names and
circumstances have been altered to protect identities.

ISBN 978-0-9830485-0-3

Published by Treeline Publishing, LLC
Boulder, Colorado, USA
treelinepublishing.com

This book is dedicated to the lost sheep who will return home to the sheep pen of which Jesus said, *"I have other sheep that are not of this sheep pen. I must bring them also. They too will listen to my voice, and there shall be one flock and one shepherd."*
John 10:16

I pray that this work would bring glory to our triune God, Father, Son, and Holy Spirit.

Nothing would satisfy me more than to hear from my readers that this book was instrumental in drawing many Muslims to the Savior.

Let this be written for a future generation,
that a people not yet created may praise the Lord!
Psalms 102:18

Acknowledgements

Special thanks to Greg Smith and Pierre Houssney for providing the structure and organization of this book. Additionally I am grateful to the following people for their help in making this book a reality:

- My son, Pierre, for your commitment, dedication, and many sleepless nights of selfless labor.
- My son, Zef, for your design, web, and technical skills that made our process more efficient.
- My son, André, for your wisdom, guidance, and conceptual support.
- My wife, Joy, for your competent editing and proofreading, as well as your loving support and encouragement.
- My daughter, Noelle, and my daughters-in-love, Vanee, Gigi, and Kate, for their prayers, support, wise counsel, and love.
- Don McCurry, for constantly challenging me to be balanced in my teaching and writing.
- Barbara Yandell, for your significant encouragement, and for forcing me to put my teachings on paper.
- My proofreaders, who labored behind the scenes along with Pierre and Greg: Tripp Martin, Pru Nagel, Joy Houssney, Mark Stephan, Kobus Erasmus, and André Houssney.

- The Horizons Staff, who have shouldered much of my work while I was writing: Tripp Martin, Todd Gunning, Cynthia Williams, Colette Correa, and all the others.

- CaraBeth Koepke, for your hours of transcribing and editing my talks and lectures.

- Some of the people who have impacted my life and made me the man I am now: George Verwer, Greg Livingstone, Hal Guffey, Nate Mirza, and Francis Schaeffer.

- Kenneth Taylor, for supporting me in my Arabic and Kurdish Bible translation work.

- Steve and Brenda George, for your significant partnership and encouragement for over two decades.

- My Board of Directors, who have admonished me to take the time to write.

- To the hundreds of students who have taught me more than I taught them.

Finally, my utmost gratitude goes to my Master, who modeled his life and ministry for us all. He alone is worthy of all praise.

Georges Houssney
Boulder, Colorado

Table of Contents

Chapter 1
Gaining a Heart for Muslims

To engage Islam, you must engage Muslims.

Islam is a man-made religious system. But Muslims are people, made by God, in his own image. Their human hearts and minds are the fields on which the powers and principalities do battle.

To engage Muslims, we must see them as people, not merely as representatives of a foreign religion, culture, or political ideology. As people, they are products of those things, but they are also husbands and wives, children and students, truck drivers and heart surgeons. They are God's lost children too, and he has given us the task of making disciples from among them, teaching them to obey everything that he has commanded. [1]

It isn't an easy task, and we must be honest about the challenges. The worldwide Church has struggled to impact Islam and Muslims. We must be honest about that too. But Jesus has given us all we need to complete our mission. He has passed on to us "all authority in heaven and earth," he has left us an example to follow, and he promised us the Holy Spirit to empower us. He appointed us as "Christ's ambassadors, as though God were making his appeal through us." [2] Why then are we shrinking back from the Great Commission and not living a life worthy of the calling? [3]

---

[1] Matthew 28:20.

[2] 2 Corinthians 5:20.

[3] Ephesians 4:1.

Until I left for college when I was eighteen years old, my world was mostly limited to the northern half of my country of birth, Lebanon. I was the product of three cultures: my mother came from the Orthodox Christian village of Rahbeh in the far northeast of the country, my father belonged to a small farming community outside the Maronite Christian town of Zgharta (where I was born in 1949), and when I was two years old my father moved the family to the predominantly Muslim city of Tripoli, on the coast of the Mediterranean Sea, just south of the Syrian border.

These three different worlds I lived in exposed me to three different worldviews: Orthodox, Maronite, and Muslim. In many ways these shaped the person that I grew up to be. In Lebanon, each of these groups is in turn splintered into smaller subgroups, with numerous sects living side-by-side (not always peacefully): Sunnis, Shiites, Alawis, Nusairis, Melkites, Jacobites, Druze, Jehovah's Witnesses, Presbyterians, Adventists, Baptists, and many others. I didn't grow up thinking deep thoughts about how all these religions related to each other. My main interests while attending my Greek Orthodox elementary school were playing soccer, earning pocket money by making and selling kites and slingshots, and picking fights with vulnerable children.

In 1958, Lebanon was plunged into a civil war that forced my family out of our rented apartment to become refugees in a distant village. The roads to my parents' hometowns were not safe. My older brother, Antoine, and I ended up spending our time in the fields, training with a regional militia. This was when my perspective toward Islam and Muslims changed. As we—merely boys—were trained to shoot guns and throw hand-grenades, I began to hear stories about Muslims massacring my Christian ancestors. Almost a century earlier, in 1860, an infamous massacre drove hundreds of thousands of Lebanese Christians—some of them my relatives—away from their homelands. My great-grandfather on my mother's side left for Brazil. Other relatives settled in West Africa, in pursuit of gold and diamonds. In fact, some of my immediate cousins were born and raised in Sierra Leone and only came to visit the homeland during summers.

The history of Christian-Muslim relations in the Middle East is full of wars and persecution of Christians by Muslims. My innocence was lost: I was nine years old, chased from our home by a civil war. Our neighborhood had been attacked by Muslims, and I was training with a militia to fight back. Resentment, verging on hatred, began to brew in my heart toward Islam and Muslims. It did not help that I hated to be disturbed at dawn by the cry of the *muazzin* (the man in the mosque calling Muslims to prayer) from screechy loudspeakers every day. I was taught that if we didn't kill Muslims they would kill us first. "Eat them for lunch before they have you for dinner," was the Arabic adage.

Eight months later, President Eisenhower intervened and sent his Marines to Lebanese shores, ending the war. We returned to our apartment in Tripoli and I joined a boy's street gang, committing vandalism and getting in fights with rival gangs. I was on my way to becoming just another Lebanese tough guy: living and scuffling with Muslims in the poorer streets of Tripoli, dreaming of my chance to avenge my family and ancestors. But that wasn't how God wanted me to engage Muslims. He interrupted my life with a better plan.

A Lebanese seminary student named Fayez Yousef George came to my neighborhood to open a mission center. He found me in the streets playing soccer and fighting with children from the neighborhood and handed me a copy of the Gospel of Matthew in Arabic. His beaming face and warm handshake left an indelible impression on me. The contrast between him and my Orthodox priest was stark. My parochial school demanded all their Orthodox students to be in church every Sunday. The list of absentees was presented to the principal on Monday mornings. I never missed one mass. I couldn't!

The Baptist mission center was just across a field from our condominium. Every Sunday at 1:45 p.m. you would find me standing in line, anxiously waiting for the doors to open at two. No one forced me to go. There was an irresistible attraction inside that simple rented apartment with a few benches and no icons, incense, candles, or priests with grandiose robes. There was a freshness to the atmosphere, a genuineness that I was not accustomed to. I experienced Christ expressed in that warm handshake and the loving smile of an ordinary, simple man who was not there to draw attention to himself. The focus was Jesus and his sacrificial redemptive work. One day brother Fayez, as he preferred to be called, told me: "Georges, even if you were the only one on earth, God loves you enough to come down and die to save you." Within a year, I was at the feet of Jesus repenting from my sin and turning over the reins of my life to him.

At the age of twelve I was born again by a touch of the Spirit of God in my heart. No area of my life could ever remain the same again. For the next two years I was passionate about learning and living out the Word of God.

When Jesus entered my life I began to view Muslims in a different light. The very day after I gave my life to Christ, a Muslim boy approached me in the street and hit me, but something within me restrained me from hitting him back. A sense of joy entered my heart, and I felt the presence of the Holy Spirit in me. I recognized that Jesus had done something radical in my inner being. As my pastor put it, "The old Georges is dead." I began to develop friendships with Muslims; in fact, my best friend Ziad was a Muslim. Interestingly, in middle school I had two good friends who had the exact same name: Yousef Mousa and Yousef Mousa were both my classmates, but one was a Maronite Christian and the other was a Palestinian Muslim. The entire population of the nearby Palestinian refugee camp was Muslim, and I often went with Yousef to visit some of our mutual friends there, many of whom I still remember, such as Mustapha Mi'ari.

But the major revolution in my heart toward Muslims came when I was fourteen. In 1964, a Volkswagen van bearing

Swiss plates parked on a narrow street in my mother's home village of Rahbeh, in the northeastern mountains of Lebanon. It was packed full of books and young Western missionaries, members of an Operation Mobilization team. They came through the village, visiting homes door to door. When they found me, we discovered that we shared a mutual love for Jesus. It was exciting for me to meet brothers who were dedicated to preaching Jesus to the unreached. I came along with them to the other houses in my village, translating for them and helping however I could. When it was time to move on to another village, I eagerly hopped in the van with my new friends. But then they took a fork in the road that made me freeze with fear. "This leads to Tikreet!" I urgently explained. "We cannot witness there, they are all Muslims!"

My Christian village, Rahbeh, and Tikreet–a tiny all-Muslim village of three thousand people–had a long-standing feud. Animosity over all sorts of issues between them had led to fights and bloodshed. The destroyed mosque in my village had been a major source of conflict. Tikreet supported rebuilding it against the will of the all-Orthodox population of Rahbe, except for three Muslim families. Any time they attempted to rebuild the mosque, a fight would break out with fists, knives, or even guns.

But there we were, parked in the center square of Tikreet, and I did not want to get out of the van. My hatred of Muslims in general made it very difficult for me to accompany the team on this outreach. I refused to go.

What I heard next changed my life. The young Swiss team leader, Ulrich Bruderer, asked me, "Why not? Didn't Jesus die for Muslims too?" I did not have an answer. Noticing my silence, he followed up with another earth-shaking question, "Georges, do you think God loves Muslims?" Then he reminded me of the verse that had impacted me the most: "For God so loved the world..."

That was all I needed to realize that even though I had been a Christian for two years and had stopped fighting Muslims, I still did not love them.

My Sunday school teacher had once inserted my name into John 3:16: "...for God so loved Georges..." But then some stranger from Switzerland came all the way to the far hills of Lebanon to teach me that God's love was not all about me. Yes, God indeed loves Georges, but God's love is much bigger than my ego, bigger than my church, bigger than my people, bigger than my country, and even bigger than the world. My understanding of God's love had been dwarfed by my immature, egocentric view of God, who until then existed just for me: to love me, save me, and serve me.

This new understanding of God's love for the whole world–for all peoples of the world–was effectively a second conversion. It shook me to the core. My hatred toward Muslims vanished. God replaced it with compassion and love. That was the day I knew deep down that God was planting a vision in my heart that was much greater than my own salvation. I began to realize that God was calling me to commit the rest of my life to loving Muslims and sharing with them the love of God that they do not know. Strangely, it had just never occurred to me that God loves Muslims. I was dumbfounded. Muslims were no longer my enemies or merely acquaintances. God was growing my love for them, and fanning my desire to bring the Gospel to as many Muslims as I could.

Every summer for the next eight years I went door-to-door with an OM team, from village to village. On foot we visited dozens of villages each month, eventually covering most of northeastern Lebanon.

Dr. Bob Jones (senior) visited Lebanon and personally offered me a scholarship to his university in America. Of course, I knew nothing about the school. Besides, I had responsibilities at several churches in Lebanon, and couldn't imagine dropping those to go to America. In 1967, the Lord opened a door for me to attend university in Beirut, where I studied psychology and psycholinguistics, with a minor in education. My entire tuition was paid by anonymous gifts. I could not have afforded it otherwise.

One semester, I signed up for an elective course on comparative religions. I could not pass up the opportunity to try to understand the great phenomenon of religion. Our professor, Dr. Richard Thomas, was born in Palestine to an Armenian mother and a Scottish father. Our first lecture was about the similarities between the religions of the Middle East. Dr. Thomas drew columns on the chalkboard to represent various religions and began to explain the variety of perspectives on common topics such as prayer, fasting, pilgrimage, etc.

I struggled with this comparative approach. It sounded like all religions were pretty much the same: they pray, they fast, and practice similar acts of kindness while attempting to please their gods. As a committed Christian, he made sure we understood that he believed in the uniqueness of Christ and the distinction between the Christian faith and all other religions. He warned us against relativism, and pointed out the dangers of studying comparative religions. It may lead to a pluralistic worldview that seeks to find similarities rather than differences.

Engaging Muslims directly with the Gospel became my goal, the vision of my heart. My college years were filled with missionary activity. I served with the Navigators, Campus Crusade, InterVarsity, and was president of Campus Christian Fellowship–all at one time. On weekends I was traveling to three different locations in North Lebanon, leading Sunday school, worship, teaching, and preaching in three churches. Nothing could stop my heart from exploding with the desire to share Christ.

By then, the Lord had prepared me for what was to come. When I was a nineteen-year-old sophomore, my OM team leader, John Ferwerda, invited me to "Love Europe." This was a door-to-door campaign in Belgium, France, and England, evangelizing Muslims from Pakistan, India, and North Africa.

Three years later, in 1971, I was on a plane heading to Saudi Arabia and Yemen. This turned out to be one of the most significant experiences of my life, as the Lord showed me the power of his Holy Spirit in war-torn Yemen. In three weeks, thirty-five Muslim men gave their lives to Christ. My only strategy was to read and explain the gospels: engaging Muslims with the story of Jesus. This experience shaped my missiology for years to come.

Years later, I was hired by a mission agency to prepare a book for Muslims explaining the Christian perspective on the Five Pillars of Islam. I found research for the book to be extremely difficult. For a long time, I could not put my finger on exactly why I was struggling so much. At times I felt alone in my thinking. The vast majority of those interested in working with Muslims were foreigners: Americans, British, Swedes, Canadians, and other Westerners. Christians in Lebanon and other Arab countries had little or no interest in reaching Muslims. Prejudice against Islam was evident in the Lebanese church, yet the Westerners around me seemed almost neutral about Islam, or even sympathetic, unaware of the heart-level dangers that lay beneath the surface of cultural forms. I struggled to find a biblical perspective on Islam.

As I began to write a Christian counterpoint to the Five Pillars, the challenge before me was to correctly articulate the differences between Islam and Christianity. I knew from my daily interactions that Muslims and Christians are worlds apart in almost every religious practice. My studies of Arabic literature–including the Qur'an and the *Hadith*, history, Islamic philosophy, and poetry–only confirmed this conclusion. But as I collected the information for that book, I was surrounded by Western Christian leaders who seemed to have a contrary viewpoint. They talked about the need to celebrate the similarities and not to emphasize the differences. Dialogue based on mutual respect became the ideal in engaging Muslims. Interfaith conferences and round-table discussions brought Muslim and Christian leaders face-to-face. I was invited to many of these in Beirut and Cairo. I always left those meetings thinking, "What is really happening here? Can't these seemingly smart Christians see that they are compromising the Gospel?" What I saw was Christians making concessions to the Muslims that they were trying to witness to.

Obviously, Western Christians and those raised in Muslim countries had a serious difference in their attitude toward Islam, and I wanted to get to the bottom of it. Ever since I was eighteen, mentors who apparently saw leadership potential in me had given me opportunities to travel and work in various parts of the world. I deeply appreciated their support and encouragement. In fact, I would not be where I am now had it not been for the Swiss missionary, Ulrich Bruderer, who was the first to challenge me to love Muslims. Americans also had a great influence on me. Mabel Summers, a Southern Baptist missionary, drove me every Sunday to three different mission centers where I was holding Sunday meetings for children and adults. Other significant leaders who have played a major role in my life included John Ferwerda, George Verwer, Greg Livingstone, Dale Rhoton, Ralph Shallis, and Francis Schaeffer. They had a passion for the world that I did not have until I met them and heard them speak and strategize. I gleaned yet another perspective on the world from each of them.

Someone recently commented, "It seems that you live out of a suitcase and on a plane." I actually live with my wife in Boulder, Colorado, where we raised four wonderful children who are all walking with God and serving him. Airplanes do rob me of my family for a good part of the year, but obeying God and his calling is extremely satisfying, and my wife and family are fully committed with me to engaging Muslims with the Gospel.

This book is a culmination of over forty years of ministry among Muslims around the world, in most of the ninety-eight countries to which I have traveled. The lessons and principles which I bring to you have come through the refiner's fire. Tears and agony characterized the first years of my ministry.

Opposition, hardships, and even beatings have taught me that the God who called us is the same one who enables us. Nothing can thwart his plans. The most difficult hardships have been the ones that came from within the missionary movement. But in all these things we are more than conquerors. The Lord has taught me that nothing restrains our God from saving, by many or by few. I have learned that without him we can do nothing, but with him there is nothing we cannot do.

Pride and stubbornness have often hindered, not helped my work. Through it all the Lord of the harvest has been gracious and compassionate, loving and forgiving. What amazes me is that the Lord has protected me from physical, emotional, and spiritual dangers when I seemed to be headed straight into them.

Let me tell you what this book is not about. It is not about bashing Islam or condemning terrorism. It is not a survey of Islamic doctrine or history. It is not a textbook on comparative religions. It is not a call to arms for the clash of civilizations, nor is it a plea to reconcile cultures.

This book is an invitation. I invite you to see Muslims as Jesus sees them and to learn from the life and teachings of Jesus how to love, serve, and witness to Muslims. When Jesus saw the crowds, he had compassion on them, for they were like sheep without a shepherd. My prayer is that after reading this book you will feel the same whenever you meet a Muslim. And I pray that you will not only gain a heart for them, but that you will step out of your comfort zone and engage Muslims by boldly sharing the love and the message of Christ.

Chapter 2
Who Muslims Are, and Who They Are Not

Who are Muslims?[1]

If you are like most people you probably have some impression of Islam, or images of Muslim faces in your mind, or ideas about what sort of people Muslims are. But pause for a moment and ask yourself: how did you form your impressions about Islam and Muslims? What are the sources of your perceptions? Have you interacted enough with Muslims on a personal level? Have you lived among Muslims in their neighborhoods? Or even walked their streets, shopped in their bazaars, visited their sick, and attended their weddings? Did you grow up with Muslims? Have you been exposed to their problems, felt their feelings, experienced their pains, laughed with those who laugh and cried with those who cry among them? Or are your impressions mostly derived from second and third-hand sources? You have heard or read that Muslims think this, or do that. And if you have formed your impressions first hand, most likely you have done so from a distance, through the lens of your own culture and lifestyle. Even in countries where Christians and Muslims live side-by-side, they still often view each other as outsiders.

---

[1] Islam and Muslim (also spelled Moslem) are Arabic words. The first refers to the religion, and the second to the person who adheres to Islam. Both come from the same etymological root which denotes surrender.

I can't forget the reaction on the face of a Lebanese Christian woman who visited Dearborn, Michigan during that city's annual Arab Festival. She was shocked to see veiled women in the streets. For a moment she was thrown off thinking that she was either in a Muslim country or in a dream. She was so uncomfortable that she was unable to handle the experience for more than a few minutes. To her, Muslims were outside her circle, they are "other."

The reality is that most Christians, especially Western Christians,[2] don't have personal relationships with Muslims. For example, consider the United States: while Muslims appear on the news every day for one reason or another, Muslims still make up only a tiny fraction of the American people. Many of those are concentrated in a few large, urban areas. Still, Muslims can be found in all fifty states of the US. Chances are, you could make friends with a Muslim whether you live in a big city, a college town, or even a rural area. While they walk our streets, shop in our malls, and study in our universities, we have so little interaction with them that Muslims all too often remain strangers and aliens to us. While Muslims are more numerous in Europe, they still represent a small but growing segment of the population.

Because of the news surrounding various cultural and military conflicts, most Western Christians learn more about Muslims from the media than they do from personal contact. Media discussions of Islam in the context of terrorism, war, and politics have raised much alarm over the demographic

---

[2] Throughout this book I use the term "Western Christians" to describe Christians who either live in, or are products of, Western Civilization and the Western Church. In other words, those belonging to churches in Western Europe, the Americas, and Australia. Eastern Orthodox, as well as various African and Asian churches have lived in closer cultural proximity to Islam, and have a very different history of engagement with Muslims.

consequences of Muslim immigration to Western nations. There is always news of some radical mosque or fiery imam fomenting jihad on the Internet. This leaves Muslims publicly exposed, but personally ignored.

And so, Muslims are an enigma for the vast majority of Western Christians, a mysterious other. They see Muslims in movies or television fiction, where they are portrayed in exaggerated stereotypes: the terrorist, the innocent victim caught between dictators and foreign invaders, the cunning international businessman, the filthy rich, etc. In recent decades, there has been an increase of sympathy for Muslims as underdogs facing corrupt Western influences, from corporate greed to Zionism. On the other hand, Hollywood has promoted a new stereotypical Muslim: the enlightened and world-wise product of an ancient and sophisticated culture from whom narrow-minded Westerners should learn. In the 1991 movie *Robin Hood: Prince of Thieves*, Robin (played by Kevin Costner) returns to England from the Crusades with a Muslim friend, Azeem (played by Morgan Freeman), who teaches the stupid and superstitious Christians about science, women's rights, and social justice. It is a truly odd piece of historic revisionism that teaches us more about Hollywood than medieval Britain.

Some Western Christians have met Muslims while traveling. They might have visited a Muslim country on a business trip or vacation, or even a short-term mission project. They probably have fond memories of a pleasant host, shared a meal with a new Muslim acquaintance, enjoyed a knowledgeable and friendly tour guide, or had a productive business meeting with Muslim colleagues. To Western eyes, these encounters had an exotic charm. They might have exchanged contact information with these Muslims, pleased that they had made a new friend.

Many Western Christians have seen Muslims in public in a city with an immigrant Muslim community. Perhaps their taxicab driver had an Arabic name, or they rode on the subway next to several men wearing Muslim robes and small hats, presumably on their way to a mosque in the city. They might have seen a young Muslim family sitting at a McDonald's. The Westerners tried not to stare, but nevertheless stole furtive glances at the mother wearing a robe and headscarf, speaking some foreign-sounding language to several small children. Watching her interact with her bearded husband, the Westerners speculated about the gender roles within the Muslim family, wondering whether the woman was happy being covered and subservient.

Some Christians have been exposed to various Christian sources intended to educate them about Islam. They might have heard dire warnings of the Islamic threat. Some Christian resources (like this book) equip Christians for missionary efforts. But no matter how good the book, video, or workshop might be it is always only a secondary source and can never replace the experience of actually engaging Muslims on a personal level.

And that is the heart of the problem: if we want to know who Muslims are, we have to get to know some Muslims. For fourteen-hundred years Muslims and Christians have lived side-by-side. They have not always been friendly neighbors. Even in the best of times a cold war has existed between Muslim nations and the West, often heating up into shooting wars and various levels of violence. The two religions have been separated by language, politics, culture, and worldviews, causing misunderstanding, mistrust, and even animosity. Some Christians, in a well-intentioned but misguided attempt to build bridges, argue that the misunderstanding has been primarily on the Christian side. Some argue that if we were more sympathetic, loving and understanding, Muslims would treat us in kind. The truth is that for most of the last fourteen centuries Muslims have known as little about Christians as the other way around.

Islam isn't going away anytime soon. Muslims are here to stay, and they are getting closer to home. In fact, there is every reason to believe that within the next hundred years–the fifteenth consecutive century in this relationship–that contact between Christians and Muslims will only increase. Globalization of trade, international students, communications and media, immigration, education, and air travel have made it inevitable that Christians and Muslims will encounter each other in ways they never have before.

Yet the bottom line is that as I write this book in 2010 the vast majority of Christians around the world don't know many, if any, actual Muslims. Christians living in the West are even less likely to engage any Muslims seriously because most of their social relationships are with other Christians or secular westerners, and most of their free time is spent at church and inside the Christian subculture. Of course the same is true for Muslims: their lifestyle and culture make it unlikely that they have any Christian friends. The odds are that, if you are a Christian living in the Americas, Europe, or Australia, you have had no substantial relationships with Muslims unless you have worked in missions or served in the military inside a Muslim country.

To make matters worse, even those of us who have interacted with Muslims are usually exposed to only a limited scope of the world of Islam. The reality is that Muslims are as widely varied as any other set of people on earth. It's too easy to generalize based on our limited experience when the full spectrum of Muslims is much broader and more diverse.

So, the answer to our original question ("Who are Muslims?") is that most of us don't really know, beyond generalities. This makes it difficult to describe them in any meaningful way–especially since Muslims around the globe are as diverse as Christians. I see Muslims as people loved by God, not because they are Muslims, but because they are his creations. When we see them as people we can love them as Jesus loved them, and as people he is calling into his kingdom.

Who Muslims Are Not

Since so few Christians have meaningful contact with Muslims, it might be helpful to dispel some common misunderstandings. The following are the top ten misconceptions about Muslims that I have encountered in my work.

1. **"Islam is a Monolithic Religion."** Actually, Islam is as diverse as Christianity. There are ethnic, national, tribal, linguistic, and sectarian differences between Muslims. Again, our perceptions are shaped by a small minority of highly visible Muslims in the media who appear to be culturally similar. In reality, Muslims can be as different from each other as a Russian Orthodox Ukrainian is from a Texas Pentecostal. Muslims around the world do not all understand or practice Islam the same way.

2. **"All Muslims are Arabs."** Surprisingly, I am sometimes asked, "Do they speak Arabic in Turkey?" There are twenty-two countries within the Arab League (Neither Iran or Turkey is among them). They spread in an arc across all of North Africa from Morocco and Mauritania in the West, to Egypt and Sudan in the East. From Syria and Iraq in the North they run south through the Arabian Peninsula, down through the eastern Horn of Africa all the way to the tiny island of Comoros, between Madagascar and mainland Africa. Despite this sprawl over a wide swath of the planet, over eighty percent of Muslims are not actually Arabs. The countries with the largest Muslim populations are India, Indonesia, Pakistan and Bangladesh–none of the top four nations with Muslim populations are Arab!

3. **"All Arabs are Muslims."** While it may be predominantly Muslim (just as America is predominantly Chris-

tian), at least ten percent of the Arab world is Christian. Some Arab countries have large minorities of non-Muslims, such as Christians, Druze, Baha'i, or Yazidi. For example, in Lebanon Christians are a minority compared to the combined total of Sunni and Shi'ite Muslims, although they outnumber either group individually. There are large minorities of Christians in Egypt, Sudan, Jordan, Syria, Iraq, and Lebanon. Many of them would call themselves Arabs, but religiously they are Catholic, Greek Orthodox, or evangelical. Yet even Muslims are largely unaware of religious diversity among Arabs. While traveling in Muslim countries, many Muslims cannot believe that I could be Lebanese and not a Muslim. Similarly, many Muslims consider any person from a Western country to be a Christian.

4. **"All People in Arab countries are Arabs."** Kurds make up one third of Iraq's population, yet they are not Arabs. Berbers are a large minority in North Africa and yet they are not Arabs. There are other ancient ethnic groups such as Chaldeans, Assyrians, Circassians, Armenians who live within Arab nations who would be offended if someone called them "Arabs." Some Christians in Lebanon prefer to trace their ancestry to the Phoenicians rather than the Arabs. Coptic Christians in Egypt do not like to be called Arabs. The Druze are their own category; they live in Lebanon, Syria, and Israel, yet they are neither Muslim nor Arab.

5. **"Muslims are Descendants of Abraham Through Ishmael."** Not completely true. What do Indonesian Muslims have in common with Saudis? What do Chinese Muslims have in common with the Iraqis? Only their adherence to Islam, just as Korean and Italian Chris-

tians have only their faith in common. The claim that Muslims are descendants of Ishmael is a common error, even among knowledgeable Christian scholars. It is ironic that many ministries to Muslims have "Ishmael" in their name when it is likely that few Arabs have any blood relationship with Ishmael. If there is such a relationship it is only through a small segment of the tribes that inhabited the Arabian Peninsula at the time of Muhammad. However, since Muhammad claimed descent from Abraham through Ishmael many, including me, accept a spiritual link between them.

6. **"Muslims are Impossible to Reach."** Actually, we are living in an era during which Muslims are coming to Christ in unprecedented numbers, through many means. This number is likely to continue to increase as the worldwide Church awakens to the vast opportunities to engage the Muslims of our time.

7. **"When Muslims Become Christians they Always Face Persecution."** This is not true of all situations. Many do face varying levels of persecution, but most of what is called persecution is no more than arguments or threats. Very few of these actually end in serious violence or death (although martyrdom of any follower of Christ is serious and tragic). This fear of persecution has paralyzed many, both Muslims and missionaries.

8. **"Muslims Hate America."** This is another exaggeration, reinforced by the media. A humorous but real story illustrates this fact. In 2007 there was an anti-American demonstration in Khartoum, the capital city of Sudan. A

Sudanese Christian from a Muslim background (CMB)[3] decided to perform an experiment on the protesters. From the back of the crowd he started a rumor that the American embassy was giving away a limited number of free visas to any Sudanese who wanted to immigrate to America. The story spread through the crowd, which quickly dispersed as the demonstrators began racing each other to the American embassy to get in line, only to discover that it was a hoax. The truth is that Muslims in many countries do have a love/hate relationship with the West. For example, on the political level many Arabs are not happy with United States policy, but a lot of them love American culture and Americans. They love our movies, our food, our computers, and our cars. They admire our language, education, freedom, and technology–even our capitalism.

9. **"Muslims Have a Negative View of Christianity."** There is some truth to this, but it's a bit more complicated than that statement makes it seem. We must make a distinction between Islam and Muslims. Of course there are Muslims who have a negative attitude toward Christianity, whether it is for political, religious, or ethnic reasons. But many of the moderates actually admire and trust Christians, often more than they trust each other. In my life among Muslims I have observed this again and again. One of my translators of the Kurdish Bible was a Muslim professor at a Baghdad uni-

---

[3] "CMB" (Christian with a Muslim Background) is now being used to replace the more well-known "MBB" (Muslim Background Believer). In a survey, dozens of former Muslims expressed that they prefer the Christian identity. In fact, many said that they want to be known simply as a Christian.

versity. When I visited her home, she pointed out to me that her maid was a Christian. She whispered: "I really do not trust a Muslim maid."

10. **"We Need to be Secretive About our Work in the Muslim World."** Not only is this false, it is counterproductive. Most Muslim cultures value courage. Secrecy is viewed as weak and deceptive. Secretive missionaries raise suspicion about their activities (are they CIA? Israeli spies?), so they get followed by secret police more than those who are open about their identity. Boldness in witness is seen as strength and honesty, and earns respect among Muslims, even if they publicly disagree and even argue emphatically.

In his sermon to the Athenian philosophers, Paul argued that, "From one man he made every nation of men, that they should inhabit the whole earth; and he determined the times set for them and the exact places where they should live. God did this so that men would seek him and perhaps reach out for him and find him, though he is not far from each one of us." [4]

As Islam itself confesses, Muslims are (as C.S. Lewis put it in the Chronicles of Narnia) "sons of Adam" and "daughters of Eve." The Bible assures us that they are image-bearers of God. But they have lost their way, and turned their ears aside from the truth to myths. [5] Just like Jesus, we reject Islam but love Muslims.

We remember that "God was reconciling the world to himself in Christ, not counting men's sins against them. And he has committed to us the message of reconciliation. We are

---

[4] Acts 17:26-27.

[5] 2 Timothy 4:4.

therefore Christ's ambassadors, as though God were making his appeal through us." [6] And we know that someday soon all the nations will cry out, "How beautiful are the very feet of those who bring good news, proclaiming peace and salvation!" [7] But to fulfill that mission we must engage Islam, and we cannot engage Islam until we engage Muslims.

---

[6] 2 Corinthians 5:19-20.

[7] Isaiah 52:7, my paraphrase.

Chapter 3
Christian Reactions to Islam

In 1982, before moving to the USA from the Middle East, I went on a speaking tour through several US states. At a church in Kansas I asked how many in the audience had ever met a Muslim. To my shock only four people, out of perhaps a thousand in the room, raised their hands. Since then, I've continued to ask that question at my speaking appearances in churches. In recent years the number has increased, and now it is not uncommon for most people in a church to raise their hands.

How is this possible when Muslims are still a statistically small fraction of the general population? There are probably a number of factors: Muslims are among the most rapidly growing minority groups in America, globalization and education have resulted in more Muslims of diverse careers and socio-economic groups, and Americans are becoming more aware of Muslims that they might have previously ignored.

A few decades ago the Muslim minority wasn't even on the radar screen for most American Christians. Today, Muslims seem to be everywhere. But they are not all the same. They live in almost every community, and come from all walks of life. They are from many ethnic backgrounds and nationalities. Some Muslim families have been in the USA for generations, and some are immigrants who have come to America as part of a chain of relatives helping each other get visas.

Muslims have entered the American consciousness so rapidly that most Christians have not had enough time to digest the phenomenon. As a result, many are still confused as to how to think, feel, and act toward Muslims. In our *Engaging Islam* training programs, my eldest son, André, teaches a class called "Reactions to Islam." Because André is bicultural he has been able to live in the skin of the ordinary Christian in America and empathize with their feelings about Islam, while also having a Middle Eastern perspective. As he has lived among and listened to Christians over the years he has realized that their responses to Muslims tend to stem from three basic reactions: fear, fury, and fascination. As André and I have compared our experiences, we have realized that Christians will never be able to effectively engage Muslims until we understand our own reactions and let God cleanse them, replacing them with his love. In this book I would like to discuss two more reactions: forgetfulness and fatigue.

Fear

Many people are afraid of Islam. Images of the Twin Towers burning and people jumping a hundred stories to their deaths are etched into their memories. They are afraid of the physical dangers that radical Islam represents: terrorist attacks, suicide bombings, kidnappings and beheadings of travelers in Muslim lands, riots, and news reports of burning cars in European cities. These fears are reinforced by images of Muslims shouting, "Death to infidels!" on television. Fear drives some Westerners to overcompensate by avoiding anything that might offend Muslims. In 2005, a Danish newspaper published a dozen editorial cartoons depicting the prophet Muhammad. Most were innocuous, but some implied a connection between Islam and terrorism. The cartoons were mild compared to the editorial cartoons that regularly criticize Western politicians, or even Christianity. But Muslims around the world reacted violently, resulting in more than one hundred deaths and attacks on buildings throughout Europe and the Middle East, including the burning of embassies. *Fatwa* [1] death sentences were issued by imams on the cartoonist, who went into hiding. Even five years later the cartoonist and his family ran to hide in a "safe room" in his home while police shot and killed a Muslim attacker attempting to carry out the *fatwa*. In 2004, Theo Van Gogh, a descendant of the famous painter's brother, was shot and stabbed to death on an Amsterdam street after making a film criticizing Muslim treatment of women. And few have forgotten the *fatwa* issued by the Iranian Ayatollah Khomeini, calling for the murder of author Salman Rushdie for his infamous book, *The Satanic Verses.*

As a result of incidents like these, many Western companies, churches, and governments bend over backwards to avoid anything that might prompt Islamic outrage. Artists, writers, filmmakers, and journalists censor themselves, afraid of saying anything that might target them for harassment or assassination. Ironically, the same artistic community that regularly defends images or statements deeply offensive to Christians–such as Andrés Serrano's famous "Piss Christ" or Chris Ofili's dung and pornography-decorated painting of the Virgin Mary, both of which were celebrated as great art–are terrified of anything that might be construed as offensive to Muslims.

In the summer of 2010, the pastor of a small Florida church wanted to make the point that the attacks of September 11 were not the work of extremists who had hijacked Islam, but were the natural result of its belief system. He announced that he would publicly burn a copy of the Qur'an. Some, even those who regarded it as an opportunistic publicity stunt, defended it as an act of free speech; Americans have

---

[1] *Fatawa (singular: fatwa)* are verdicts pronounced by a Muslim religious leader, called a *mufti*. Some *fatawa* are just legal opinions, others are calls to *jihad* (struggle, or holy war) against enemies of Islam.

gotten used to flag burnings or desecration of Christian religious symbols. But others considered the Qur'an burning as an intolerable insult to Islam. There was an outcry by Muslims and Christians alike. Government officials in Washington and around the world predicted widespread and violent reaction from Muslims and put pressure on the pastor, who canceled his Qur'an burning ceremony. While Christians rejected the Qur'an burning as an act that didn't reflect Christ's character, too much of the popular culture reaction was tainted by fear of potential Muslim reprisals.

Many Westerners are frightened by the thought of Islam overwhelming Western societies. Muslim immigration is dramatically altering the demographics and public culture of Western Europe. Many fear that Muslims are not "regular" immigrants, but advocates of separate, Sharia-based[2] communities that will compete with the host nation's culture and government, rather than assimilating into it.

Fear has paralyzed the missionary community in many Muslim countries. This fear has dire spiritual consequences for Christians trying to engage Muslims and fulfill the Great Commission.[3] They become secretive about their identity as Christians and their commitment to the Gospel. Fearful Christians traveling or working among Muslims conceal their faith. They don't tell Muslims around them who they are or what they are doing. They tone down their witness. Christians who are afraid of offending Muslims water down the Gospel

---

[2] Sharia is an Arabic word for law. It refers to Islamic law which is based on the Qur'an and other holy books of Islam. Sharia composes a complete system of law for Islamic society.

[3] "Therefore go and make disciples of all nations, baptizing them in the name of the Father and of the Son and of the Holy Spirit, and teaching them to obey everything I have commanded you. And surely I am with you always, to the very end of the age" (Matthew 28:19-20).

and hesitate to tell Muslims that they are sinners in need of salvation. They are afraid to present the truth that Jesus is the Son of God, that he died for their sins, and that unless Muslims turn to Christ they will not be saved. They fail to heed Jesus' principle that, "No one lights a lamp and hides it in a jar or puts it under a bed. Instead, he puts it on a stand, so that those who come in can see the light."[4]

Fury

Many Westerners, including Christians, are angry at Muslims for acts of aggression against the West. They see the history of Islam as a series of continual wars of conquest waged against infidels. The Islamic invasions of the Middle East, Africa, Europe, and Asia are burned into the West's cultural memory, and modern events have reopened these wounds. Many are angry about Islamic terrorism, from the 1972 Munich Olympics through 9-11, or whatever atrocity happened last week. Many non-Muslims around the world, including Christians, find it easier to be enraged than engaged with Muslims.

They are also furious over what they see as deceptive and unfair tactics by Muslims. They feel that Muslims are attempting to subvert Western society through immigration and political manipulation. The 2010 attempt to build an "Islamic community center" a short distance from Ground Zero (the site of the collapsed Twin Towers) in New York City was seen as a provocative gesture, and polls indicated that most Americans deeply resented it. Even the center's originally proposed name, "The Cordoba House," evoked the Islamic conquest of Spain. Similar fury has erupted over plans to build a 70,000 seat "mega-mosque" in London, and resulted in France recently making it illegal for Muslim women to wear face-covering veils in public.

---

[4] Luke 8:16.

Christian anger leads to strife with Muslims. It desires to defeat Muslim arguments and humiliate Muslim apologists. It delights in the failure of Muslim leaders and symbols. It cheers for the destruction of anything Islamic, or any product of Islamic culture. Anger manifests itself as an argumentative spirit when talking with Muslims. It ought to go without saying that Christians who are furious with Muslims cannot be effective ambassadors for Christ.

Fascination

Some Christians are so curious about Islam that they become enchanted by its complexity and "otherness." Many missionaries, trying to fit into Muslim countries, get wrapped up in studying its culture and doctrines and don't realize that their study has progressed to fascination. They come to admire and sympathize with Muslims, not as people lost in a false religion but as heirs of a worthy tradition and members of a rich culture. They become impressed with Muslim devotion and zeal for God, contrasting it to the apparent laxity of many Christians. Indeed, on the surface, Islamic worship does seem admirable: millions of Muslims wake up at dawn to do their ritualistic washings, spread a prayer carpet, and bend their knees to Allah.[5] The name of Allah is always on their lips. They appear pious and are willing to die for their religion. Some fascinated Christians begin to convince themselves that we all worship the same God, and that while the Qur'an and the Bible do not agree about everything there is still enough common ground to build spiritual bridges to Muslims. This sort of rationalized fascination results in avoiding any form of

---

[5] "Allah" is the Arabic word for "God", which is used by both Christians and Muslims, although they have two completely different concepts of God. In this book, both words ("God" and "Allah") may be used for both conceptions of God (Muslim and Christian).

confrontation that may offend or push away Muslims and jeopardize future engagement.

For those Christians who are bored with or ashamed of Western civilization–or even Christianity itself–Islam offers an exotic, non-Western alternative to their own heritage. They become intoxicated by a mythical Islamic past, which Muslim sources (and increasingly Western as well) describe as more glorious and enlightened than the familiar but grubby details of Christian history.

Other Christians, tired of conflict and wounded by what they perceive as mean-spirited attacks against Muslims, feel sympathy for this group of maligned people. When exposed to the often admirable social and family traditions of Muslims, and the apparent sincerity of their faith, these Christians often tend toward solidarity with Muslims.

Unfortunately, Western culture has largely eliminated sacred devotion and liturgical practice from daily life. Starved for tangible spirituality, many in the West cannot bring themselves to re-embrace Christianity–perhaps familiarity really does breed contempt. And so for decades Westerners have been drawn to foreign examples of spiritual practice such as Hindu yoga or the devotion of Buddhist monks in Tibet. Increasingly, they are enchanted by the devotional practices of Islam: Westerners who struggle to pray a few minutes a week are impressed by Muslims who pray five times a day. For such people, Islamic culture appears untainted by the modernity and commercialization that characterizes much of Western religion. Even devout Christians who live in Muslim countries for business, NGO-projects, or missionary work can become fascinated with Islamic culture and begin to embrace its religious premises.

This flirting with Islam leads to *syncretism,* the fusion of different belief systems. Syncretizing Christian and Muslim worldviews leads to blind spots in evangelism and hesitancy to rebuke sin in Muslim behavior. Becoming overly enamored with Islamic devotion leads to legalism, and can make Christians feel "unspiritual" because their faith doesn't prescribe similarly rigorous practices. Fascination with Islamic theology muddies the clarity and simplicity of the Gospel, the very Gospel of which Paul said that he was not ashamed, "because it is the power of God for the salvation of everyone who believes: first for the Jew, then for the Gentile."[6]

Forgetfulness

Some Christians don't want to think about Islam at all. Whether they know anything about it or not, and regardless of whether they have generally positive or negative impressions of Muslims, they simply do not want to have to confront the reality that Islam is growing in size and influence. Apathy is a common attitude, and often a psychological defense when we feel overwhelmed by life. Most Americans are too busy with their own lives to bother with building relationships with Muslims. In our ministry to international students I have tried in vain, year after year, to get churches to provide friendship partners for Muslim students. Even the few individuals in the churches who do sign up to become friendship partners often do not follow through. Are they heartless? Do they not care? I cannot judge their hearts but their actions clearly show indifference. In Boulder, Colorado–home of the University of Colorado–we have over a hundred students from Saudi Arabia each year. Yet almost none of them have a relationship with an American family. They tend to cluster around each other. Why? Is it because they are not interested in Americans? Perhaps some are not, but most are wide open and even seek friendship with Americans–when they arrive in the USA. But after two or three weeks they begin to gravitate toward one another. At first, many avoid the mosque and other Muslims who may pressure them to be religious. Most of them are not particularly religious and came to America hoping for a more

---

[6] Romans 1:16.

secular experience. If they do not form meaningful relationships with their American peers, after a while they give up and begin going to the mosque to find belonging and acceptance. They cannot imagine Americans accepting them, so they push away and revert into their comfort zone. Ironically, this experience often causes them to become more Islamic in America than they were in Saudi Arabia, although many of them take full advantage of the moral freedom they have while in the West. They represent a lost opportunity: Americans who worry about Muslim extremism could have introduced them to relationships with Christians that would have opened doors to salvation.

The irony is that I know a number of churches that pray for the Muslim world and ask God to save Muslims and change Muslim countries. And yet these same churches are unwilling to reach out across the street or across town to the millions of Muslims who live and study among us. It is a shame. If this is not apathy, what is it?

Fatigue

To be honest, some are tired of hearing about Muslims. They are exhausted by the "Religion of Perpetual Outrage" that we hear about in the news. Muslims always seem to be chanting and waving fists on television. They always seem to be complaining about some discrimination or offense that has supposedly been inflicted upon them. They seem to always be angry about something, whether it's the lack of halal food in prisons or a yoghurt package that resembles "Allah" in Arabic. Some of us paid no attention to Muslims at all before 9-11, and now we can't turn on a TV, or read a paper, or go to church without hearing about them, their demands, or what we are supposed to do for them. Floods in Pakistan? "Times are tough all over," we think. We'd rather support relief work in Haiti or go on a mission trip to Guatemala: we figure that at least those people don't want to blow us up. We never hear Buddhists going on and on about their grievances, or rhapsodizing on YouTube about how they are going to triumph over our civilization. Frankly, some of us don't want to hear any more about Muslims. To use a term from media or marketing, Muslims are currently "overexposed."

Fatigue leaves no room for compassion, or for us to look beyond their religious identity and see Muslims as individuals. As someone who has dedicated his life to motivating and training Christians to share the Gospel with Muslims, I'm quite familiar with the withdrawn body language and glazed-over eyes of Christians who don't want to be told that they should pay attention to the Muslims in their midst. Sometimes the more we say about Islam, the less some people care about the issue. I recognize that an orphaned child in Ethiopia or the family losing their home down the block are more sympathetic figures for ministry. And yet the increased visibility of Islam in the world is evidence that God has made missions to Muslims one of the great challenges and opportunities of our time.

Boldness, Gentleness, and Truth

All of these reactions (fear, fury, fascination, forgetfulness, and fatigue) lead us to engage Muslims in unhealthy and ineffective ways (secrecy, strife, syncretism, apathy, and exhaustion). The proper Christian reaction to lost people is love. The love of Christ should fill us with boldness, gentleness, and truth, as well as involvement and action.

Fear leads to secrecy, but love casts out fear, and produces boldness for the Gospel. 1 John 4:17-18 tells us that, "In this way, love has been made perfect among us, that we may have boldness...There is no fear in love; but perfect love casts out fear." If we do not present the Gospel boldly and clearly, what good are we as Jesus' followers? Jesus said that since salt which has lost its saltiness is no longer good for anything, and that since a light on a hill cannot be hidden we should let our light shine before men[7]. Will that sometimes result in danger for Christians when cultures that stand opposed to Christ are engaged? Of course it will. Did we expect that following a crucified savior would always be safe?[8]

Fury over past aggression leads to strife, but love melts fury and leads to gentleness. Paul instructs Timothy that, "the Lord's servant must not quarrel; instead, he must be kind to everyone, able to teach, not resentful."[9] We cannot be faithful servants of the Gospel if we are motivated by anger, much less rage. The sentiments in the hymn "Onward Christian Soldiers" are understandable and inspirational. But the metaphor of carrying the Gospel to Muslims as if we were going to war does not capture the proper motivation for missionary work, which ought to be a bold gentleness (a paradox that only Christ can model for us). We must engage Muslims with love and without arguing, and patiently explain the good news that Christ commissioned us to bear.

Fascination leads to syncretism, so that we no longer have a distinct Gospel. But the love of God teaches us all things. It teaches us to love the true Gospel, instead of letting it become polluted with myths and false religions. "Speaking the truth in love, we will in all things grow up into him who is the Head, that is, Christ."[10] Ever since Adam and Eve fell for the serpent's half-truths,[11] mankind's understanding has been darkened.[12] The Gospel is not a "cleverly invented story,"[13] but

---

[7] Matthew 5:13-16.

[8] John 15:20.

[9] 2 Timothy 2:24.

[10] Ephesians 4:15.

[11] Genesis 3.

[12] Romans 1:21.

[13] 2 Peter 1:16.

an eyewitness account of the truth that shall set us free. [14] We must resist the temptation to water down the Gospel or fuse it with Islam, no matter how charming or inspirational some of its traditions can be.

Healthy Attitudes Toward Muslims

We talked about the misperceptions we have of Muslims, and the unhealthy reactions we have to Islam. But how *should* we think and feel toward these people who are strangers to most Christians? What are healthy attitudes that we can bring to our engagement with them?

First of all, we must see Muslims as individuals, and distinguish between Islam as a system and Muslims as people. God determined the times and places where all of us are born. [15] Therefore God has ordained that many Muslims would be products of Islamic cultures where they have had little or no exposure to Christianity. They are products of their culture and environment, just as we are. This does not argue for relativizing the truth, but it should fill us with compassion and understanding for the individual men, women, and children that we encounter in Muslim communities. More than that, it means that God has given us (the Church) the seemingly impossible task of sharing his Gospel with each one of them.

Second, a healthy attitude recognizes both the good and bad in Islam and Muslims. People are confused when they hear two contradictory messages about Islam. There are those who say it is violent, and that Muslims want to destroy all infidels. On the other hand, there are those who go out of their way to argue that Islam is a religion of peace, a victim of the radical factions twisting its message. There is always a tempta-

---

[14] John 8:32.

[15] Acts 17:26.

tion to polarize issues, pigeonholing things into extreme categories. We need to face the fact that Islam has two elements: one peaceful and one at war with the world. The Qur'an has both peaceful teachings and teachings that command the faithful to destroy non-Muslims. We should be honest about both realities.

Third, we must love Muslims while hating the lies that keep them in captivity. That sounds extreme to post-modern ears, which have been taught to respect all religions. But Islam is a false gospel, and Muhammad was a false prophet who claimed that Jesus did not die on the cross to save us from our sins. The Bible teaches that, "There is no name under heaven, other than that of Jesus Christ, by which men may be saved." [16] How can we value a religion which leads so many people away from eternal life? It is possible to respect people without agreeing with their belief system. It is also possible to respect certain elements of the cultural heritage of Muslim peoples (who cannot be moved by the art and architecture of the Islamic palace of the Alhambra in Granada, Spain?), while rejecting the false revelation of the Qur'an. The Qur'an contains biblical characters and stories, but they are all twisted, creating powerful strongholds against the truth in the minds of Muslims. Paul wrote, "The weapons we fight with are not the weapons of the world. On the contrary, they have divine power to demolish strongholds. We demolish arguments and every pretension that sets itself up against the knowledge of God, and we take captive every thought to make it obedient to Christ. And we will be ready to punish every act of disobedience, once your obedience is complete." [17] Notice that Paul's goal is "to punish every act of disobedience," by seeing the sinners' restoration through obedience. In the same way we

---

[16] Acts 4:12.

[17] 2 Corinthians 10:4-6.

must hope to see Islam condemned as Muslims are saved from it.

Fourth, a healthy attitude sees the lostness of Muslims with a heart of compassion, not contempt. There is far too much anger among Christians. It is understandable but not excusable. Yes, there have been too many terrorist acts against Christians. Yes, Sharia law, based on the Quran[18] and the *Hadith*, declares *jihad* (war) against Christians and Jews. Yes, Christians in Muslim lands are second-class citizens, denied promotion and other opportunities and rights. Yes, there is continual pressure on them to abandon their faith. Yes, converts are sentenced to death. Etcetera, etcetera, etcetera. There is much evil in Islam. And yet Jesus prayed that the Father would forgive the Roman soldiers (products of another false religion) who nailed him to the cross, for they did not know what they were doing.[19] We are called to love Muslims, and bless those who persecute us.[20] This is unambiguous in the New Testament.

Fifth, we are to be innocent as doves, yet shrewd as snakes.[21] Jesus has sent us out among enemies. He instructs us to love our enemies, but still understand the dangers in living among them. A healthy attitude is alert to risks, being wise and careful stewards of our lives and opportunities, without being fearful.

Finally, a healthy attitude recognizes that Muslims need Christ. Islamic devotion, no matter how regular or intense, is not a substitute for faith in Christ as the only savior and Lord. Their piety is not enough to please God. They cannot save

---

[18] Most famously, Qur'an 9:29, among others.

[19] Luke 23:24.

[20] Romans 12:14.

[21] Matthew 10:16.

themselves by climbing the Five Pillars of Islam [22] to heaven. Their recognition of Jesus as a prophet is not enough. Their belief in God's existence and even in other fragments of truth must not blind us to this fact: no matter how religious, pious, or even well-behaved Muslims are, they still are lost without Christ.

---

[22] In Sunni Islam, the Five Pillars are *Shahada* (the Confession), *salat* (prayers), *zakat* (alms-giving) *sawm* (Fasting), and *hajj* (Pilgrimage).

Chapter 4
The Religious Life of Muslims

In the early 1990s, I was delivering a talk about Islam at Cherry Hills Community Church in South Denver. In the audience of more than a thousand people were thirty Muslims, accompanied by their imam. Afterward, the Pakistani imam invited me to his house to discuss the contents of my lecture. During the four-hour visit we talked about the differences between Christianity and Islam. As I shared my testimony and how Jesus had transformed my life, he interrupted me. "My business is not to believe or understand anything," he said with great passion. He paused for a moment, then asserted, "As a Muslim I am commanded to obey and do Allah's bidding." He did not want to hear about the possibility of a personal and intimate relationship with God. When I asked him what God expected of him, he did not hesitate to name the "Five Pillars of Islam." [1]

This reminded me of my military training in Lebanon. The trainer told us over and over that, "In military service you obey, no questions asked." This is how it is with Muslims. All they know is that they are supposed to practice certain required rituals.

Muhammad, the Prophet of Islam, is said to have instituted these religious rituals with this saying from the *Hadith*: [2]

---

[1] This book describes the Five Pillars according to Sunni Islam. The Shiite Five Pillars are quite different, made up of abstract concepts rather than deeds.

[2] *Hadith* are narrated traditions about the life and sayings of Muhammad that are secondary in authority to the Qur'an.

"Islam has been built upon five things: on [confessing] that there is no god save Allah, and that Muhammad is his Messenger; on performing *salat*; on giving the *zakat*; on *hajj* to the House; and on fasting during Ramadan."[3] Therefore what makes one a Muslim is the practice of the Five Pillars of *deen* (religion). They are *Shahada, salat, sawm, zakat,* and *hajj* (the Confession, prayer, fasting, almsgiving, and pilgrimage).

The First Pillar of Islam: *Shahada* (the Confession)

The first pillar of Islam is the *Shahada* (confession). Every Muslim is required to testify that Allah is the only God and that Muhammad is his prophet. Both elements are equally necessary, as one imam emphasized at an event on the University of Colorado campus in Boulder. The Muslim Student Association had sponsored a lecture explaining Islam. As I was leaving, the imam of the local mosque ambushed me at the door. We had talked several times before, and he knew of my background and work. As if he were trying to impress his out-of-town guest speaker, he called me over and asked, "Are you now ready to become a Muslim?"

"What do I have to do to become a Muslim?" I replied.

"All you have to do," the imam countered, "is to repeat after me these words: *La Ilaha Illa Allah and...*"

I interrupted, "I believe that there is only one God." I smiled, for surely we could agree on that.

But the imam countered, because it wasn't that simple. "Ah, but you have to also confess the second part, that Muhammad is his prophet."

"I do not believe that Muhammad is God's prophet," I replied, honestly.

"Well then," said the imam, his point proven, "you are not ready to become a Muslim."

---

[3] On the authority of Abu 'Abd al-Rahman 'Abdullah bin 'Umar bin al-Khattab. [Hadiths Al-Bukhari & Muslim].

What the imam wanted me to do was recite the *Shahada*, the first pillar of Islam: "There is no god but Allah, and Muhammad is his messenger."

In fact, anyone entering Islam has to only recite the *Shahada* to become a Muslim.

There is a humorous story which made it to the front pages of many Arab newspapers in 1972. Moammar Qaddafi, the ruler of Libya, sponsored an interfaith dialogue conference and invited both Christian and Muslim leaders. A Catholic bishop stood up and recited the *Shahada* as part of his speech comparing Christianity with Islam. The next morning, newspapers throughout the Arab world declared on their front pages that this Lebanese Catholic bishop had converted to Islam. The very fact that he had recited the words–even in the context of a speech contrasting the two religions–led Muslims to believe that he was a Muslim. Ironically, Muslims treat the *Shahada* as an action even though it is a statement of belief. In other words, simply saying it–regardless of one's level of conviction–is good enough to qualify one as a believer. It took months for the bishop to clear his name.

The *Shahada* has a powerful impact on Muslims throughout their lives. It is whispered in the ears of every Muslim when they are born and on their deathbed. Every day of his life a Muslim is supposed to repeat the *Shahada* again and again, like a mantra. Five times a day, from dawn to bedtime it echoes across the city from loudspeakers atop the minarets as a part of the call to prayer. Muslims utter the *Shahada* throughout the day in regular conversation.

In contrast, evangelical Christianity expects those who come to Christ to understand the Gospel, not merely to recite it. It is by grasping and affirming it with all our heart that we open ourselves to the redeeming work of Christ. Evangelical Christians are encouraged to ask questions and learn as much as they can about their faith. Christian testimony is about witnessing to the transforming work of Christ in our lives. We are commanded by God not to utter the name of God in vain, [4] and Jews use the phrase *ha-shem* (the name) every time the word *YHWH* (also un-voweled out of reverence) comes up in the text, for fear of disobeying this commandment. In contrast, Muslims are encouraged to utter the name Allah and his ninety-nine names constantly.

The Second Pillar of Islam: *Salat* (Prayer)

Next to the *Shahada*, *salat* (prayer) is the most commonly practiced pillar. Each Muslim is supposed to perform five prayers every day at prescribed times using prescribed words.

Even though I grew up in a Muslim city, because we were Christians I was fourteen before I first observed an Islamic prayer up close. I was at our neighbors' house to visit with their son, Ali. At a particular time his mother rose from her futon on the floor and went to the bathroom. She was uttering some words under her breath.

"My mother is now going to pray," said Ali.

I was puzzled. "Why is she going to pray in the bathroom?"

"My mother is not going to pray in the bathroom," Ali giggled. "She is going to do the *wudu'* (washings) and then pray."

By the time he was finished explaining it to me she was already out of the bathroom. She returned to the living room carrying a prayer rug.

I must have looked confused, because Ali continued to explain. "Muslims use a prayer rug to help them stay focused. Since they are supposed to always face the *Kaaba* [5] in Mecca when they pray, the rug helps my mom not to lose her direction."

---

[4] Deuteronomy 5:11.

[5] The *Kaaba* is a black, cubical building in Mecca, Saudi Arabia, that is the most sacred site of Islam. Before Islam it housed hundreds of idols, but is now where Muslims around the world direct their prayers.

We quietly watched his mother go through the motions of prayer. She stood, bowed, and kneeled, whispering some words. She repeated the routine several times. Ali leaned over and whispered, "My mom is reciting the fatiha and other verses from the Qur'an."

When she was about done with her prayers, Umm Ali ("mother of Ali") turned her face to the right then to the left each time saying in a clear voice, "*Assalamu 3alaykum.*" [6]

I knew those words. This is how Muslims greet one another. I was puzzled. "Why is she doing that?" I asked.

Ali was surprised how little I knew about Islam. "There are two angels who sit on our shoulders," he scolded me. "They are the recording angels. One keeps track of the good deeds and the other the bad ones." I was just about to ask why they do that when he continued, "This is how Allah decides whether we go to heaven or hell." He went on to explain that at death the recording angels surrender their books to be weighed by God on the Day of Judgement.

This was all very different from my own newly-formed understanding of prayer. I had just given my life to Christ two years before and it had changed my world. Although I had seen Muslims pray from a distance I was not interested in what that actually involved. I had just taken everything for granted without asking questions. But that summer I began to sense God's calling to dedicate the rest of my life to reaching Muslims for Christ. I began to pay attention to the Muslims around me in a new way, and tried to understand the differences between their religion and my own.

I was passionate about the Lord as a new convert. I read the Bible unceasingly and never missed a meeting in our little church of twenty members in Tripoli, Lebanon. Every day the

---

[6] The number "3" is commonly used in the Arab world to represent the Arabic letter "ain" (ع) in Latin script. I have chosen to include it in certain instances, to aid Arabic learners in correct pronunciation.

Muslim call to prayer echoed from loudspeakers throughout the city, but we Christians always had something of our own: worship, Bible studies, prayer meetings, and social events.

Then and now, prayer has always been an intimate relationship with God for me, not a ritual I must perform. When talking with my heavenly father, it doesn't enter my mind that it could earn me credit as a good deed. God's Holy Spirit is present when we pray and there is a connection between the human and the divine. What a great difference that is from the obligations of Islam! And not only a difference, but a gift, privilege, and opportunity from our creator and savior.

The Third Pillar of Islam: *Sawm* (Fasting)

Only the first and second pillars are practiced daily. *Sawm* (fasting) is practiced once a year during the month of Ramadan, which is the ninth month of the year in the Muslim lunar calendar. It involves abstinence from eating, drinking, smoking, and sexual intercourse from sunrise to sunset. During this time Muslims typically sleep during the day and feast at night. In fact, whatever you deny yourself during the day you can indulge in through the night. The fast is broken with an elaborate feast. In some Muslim cities, cannons are fired to mark the commencement of Ramadan, as well as the breaking of the fast at every sunset throughout the month.

Tradition has it that the descent of the Qur'an occurred on the *Laylatul Qadr*[7] ("Night of Power") during one of the last nine days of Ramadan. Muslims increase their devotion during these days and try to read the entire Qur'an as many times as they can. My neighbor Fatima probably never prayed all year, and she did not read the Qur'an or practice any religious act. Yet when Ramadan came, she was as religious as

---

[7] *Laylatul Qadr* is described in the 97th Sura (chapter) of the Qur'an, "Al Qadr," which is five verses long.

could be. She fasted from sunrise to sunset, read the Qur'an daily, and listened to religious programming on the radio.

According to one *hadith*, Muhammad said that, "Ramadan is a month whose beginning is mercy, whose middle is forgiveness and whose end is freedom from the hellfire." And, "When the month of Ramadan starts, the gates of heaven are opened and the gates of hell are closed and the devils are chained." [8]

In many Muslim nations, fasting during Ramadan is enforced by police who roam the streets. Almost everything shuts down, making it pointless for people to move around anyway. So many just stay home and sleep through the day and come out at night. The month of fasting can more accurately be called the month of feasting.

The Fourth Pillar of Islam: *Zakat* (Almsgiving)

While Christians are supposed to give one tenth of their income to the work of God, Muslims are required to give two-and-a-half percent, or one fortieth, of all surplus wealth (above an exempted amount). This money goes to Islamic causes including the mosque, the poor, and for those fighting for Islam. Any extra money contributed would be purely voluntary. Giving of alms earns Muslims more credit with God and can cancel out some of their sins.

The Fifth Pillar of Islam: *Hajj* (Pilgrimage)

There was much commotion outside our house. From my balcony I watched Umm Samir ("mother of Samir") being carried on a stretcher. I immediately assumed that she was ill and was being taken to the hospital. When I joined the neighborhood crowd I heard a woman whispering to another, "Umm Samir will never come back from Mecca." Years later I learned

---

[8] Bukhari Book #31, hadith #123.

that dying on the pilgrimage is said to be one of the surest ways to go to heaven.

Pilgrimage to Mecca is perhaps the greatest goal in Islamic life. It is required of every pious Muslim once in their lifetime, provided that they are physically and financially able. Some of the requirements of the *hajj* are to perform ceremonial ablutions, to wear two seamless tunics, to kiss the Black Stone, to circumambulate the *Kaaba* seven times, to drink from the well of Zemzem, to run between the hills of Safa and Marina in imitation of Hagar, to visit the plain of Arafat, to throw stones at the "First," "Middle," and "Great Devil" pillars, and to make animal sacrifices. Hundreds–and in some years thousands–of pilgrims die during the pilgrimage due to heat and being trampled by the stampede of two million pilgrims. But some Muslims have other fears about the *hajj*.

I will never forget how fearful my Pakistani friend Hussein was before he traveled to Mecca. He had planned to stop over in Mecca on his way home after completing his education in Boulder, Colorado. He disclosed to me his fear of this once-in-a-lifetime experience. "Every *hajji* (pilgrim) I have known in Pakistan is corrupt. It seems that they come back worse than they went." He explained to me that they wear white robes the rest of their lives and put on white caps to identify them as holy *hajjis*. He observed that they begin to exploit people and indulge in fortune-telling. "While they are viewed by the public as saints, there is nothing saintly about them," he concluded. His fear of becoming corrupted by the holiest experience of his life confirmed my conviction that this experience is demonic. I had spent hours with Hussein every week for ten months, studying the Bible. He began to gain spiritual insights. I pointed out to him that the *Kaaba* and the black stone are idols and therefore he could be exposing himself to demonic powers. I appealed to him to cry out to Jesus while there to protect him from the evil spirits. He took me seriously, but I never heard from him again.

The Six Articles of *Iman* (Belief)

Muslim scholars identify six articles of *iman* (belief) that must be affirmed. These are taken from a *hadith* in which Muhammad, the prophet of Islam, defined *iman*. "That you affirm your faith in Allah, in his angels, in his books, in his apostles, in the Day of Judgement, and you affirm your faith in the divine decree about good and evil." [9]

A Muslim is not required to have an in-depth understanding of these six articles of belief. He is not drilled on his comprehension of them. All Muslims are expected to be able to recite and affirm the list, no matter how superficial their knowledge may be. The Allah of Islam is to be appeased and obeyed, not known personally.

The First Article of *Iman*: Belief in Allah

Muslims must acknowledge that God exists and accept that he is one. This doctrine, called *tawhid,* stresses Allah's oneness or singularity. God is thought of as an arithmetic unity. This idea arose in opposition to the polytheism practiced by the Meccans and Bedouins of Muhammad's day, and the so-called "heretical trinitarian" views that Muhammad heard expounded among the Christian sects. God is also thought of as transcendent, separate from his creation, aloof, impersonal, omnipotent, and omniscient, although merciful. A mutual relationship between man and Allah is therefore impossible. He is indescribable in terms of any human characteristics. He is without emotions. He is beyond morality, unbound by the moral code he himself created, since he meant it only for humans, and is himself the author of both good and evil. Along these lines, he is also considered to be arbitrary, capricious, and unpredictable.

---

[9] Sahih Muslim Book 1, #1.

The Second Article of *Iman*: Belief in the Angels (*Mala'ika*)

Angels are, according to Islamic doctrine, reasoning beings that were created from light. There is a hierarchy within their ranks. At the top are Gabriel, who supposedly transmitted the Qur'an to Muhammad, Asrafel, who on the Day of Judgement will sound the trumpet, and Azrael, the angel of death. The lesser angels are assigned to individual humans. Each person has two recording angels who write down his or her deeds; one angel is assigned to record the good deeds, the other the bad deeds.

Also attached to each individual is a *qarina*, a person's demonic equal. The *qarina* is born with every child, and its purpose is to haunt and distract people from the straight path. Also evil (for the most part) are the *jinn*, who are spirits created from fire. Some of these Jinn are believed to be Muslim, and Muhammad claimed to have converted his *qarina* to Islam. [10] The ultimate evil being is *Shaytan* (Satan), who is an angelic being. [11] Belief in these angels and spirits causes superstition and fear in many Muslims. This leads to the use of amulets and charms, superstitiously invoking the name of Allah, and the like.

The Third Article of *Iman*: Belief in Allah's Books (*Kutub*)

Islam recognizes four major holy books: the *Tawrat* (Torah), the *Zabur* (Psalms), the *Injeel* (Gospel), and the Qur'an (Recitation). The Qur'an says these books were given to Moses, David, Jesus, and Muhammad, respectively. This reflects the simplistic Islamic concept that each prophet was given a book, and also that seemingly every biblical character

---

[10] Sahih Muslim, Book #039, hadith #6759. Versions in Arabic differ between Muhammad saying "*fa aslamu*" (and I am safe from [the *qarina*]) and "*fa aslama*" (and [the *qarina*] became Muslim).

[11] Qur'an, Sura 7:11-16.

mentioned in the Qur'an is called a prophet. Not much explanation is given as to where the rest of the prophets' heavenly books are, or what they are called. Regardless, the Qur'an is claimed to be the last and greatest of the books, and Muhammad the last and greatest of the prophets. Although the Qur'an affirms the books before it, it contradicts them on many points, leading Muslims to believe that the previous books had been corrupted at some point by the Jews and Christians.

The Qur'an is claimed to be uncreated, eternal (which means it existed before the creation of the world), and final. Its contents abrogate (cancel out) all preceding scriptures, and (as any Muslim will tell you) everything from the previous books is recorded (*mazkur*) or collected (*mjamma3*) in the Qur'an. The Qur'an is therefore the only book that is actually respected. After all, after the Qur'an had been given all the others became unnecessary, and would be so even if they had not been corrupted. However, the "uncorrupted," supposedly nonexistent forms of the prior heavenly books are all honored in the Qur'an.

The Fourth Article of *Iman*: Belief in the Prophets (*Anbiyaa'*)

In Islam, a prophet is a messenger to whom Allah has communicated a message to his subjects. They are gifted with both piety and leadership ability. All prophets are also thought to be infallible (*ma3soom*). Although many scholars admit that prophets have made "mistakes," they are not regarded as "sins." They are not, however, thought to be endowed with supernatural abilities like seeing the future. Islam claims that Allah has sent 124,000 prophets altogether.[12] Muslim scholars claim that "Every known nation has had one prophet or more...They were prepared and chosen by God to deliver his mes-

---

[12] Musnad Ahmad Ibn Hanbal #21257.

sage to mankind." [13] Twenty-five of these are mentioned in the Qur'an, most from the Jewish and Christian scriptures. Of these twenty-five, six are considered major prophets: Adam, Noah, Abraham, Moses, Jesus, and Muhammad. Muhammad, unlike all other nationalistic prophets, became the "seal of prophets," the only one who came not to just one nation but to the whole world.

The Fifth Article of *Iman*: Belief in the Day of Judgement (*Yawm el Hisaab*)

The Day of Judgement is a concept prominent in the early preaching of Muhammad. There will be a resurrection of the dead and a final judgement, from which people will be sent either to heaven or to hell. The destiny of each individual on that day is determined either by works or by the foreordination of Allah. It is unclear which of these will determine one's fate because Muhammad's earlier preaching, meant to inspire fear in his opponents in Mecca, espoused judgement by works. However, his later preaching, which promised eternal life to believers in this new religion, espoused judgement by foreordination.

The Sixth Article of *Iman*: Belief in Predestination (*Qadaa' wa Qadar*)

The belief that all things, good or bad, are foreordained by the unchangeable decrees of Allah leads Muslims to a denial of human responsibility. When a child is sick, or a car accident occurs, or even a natural disaster takes place the typical response of a Muslims is, "It is written." That means God had preordained it to happen and nothing could stop it. Sometimes Muslims do not take their sick to the hospital lest they interfere with God's will.

---

[13] Abdalati, Hammudah, 'Islam in Focus.' p. 30-31.

In Islam, true religion is resignation to the divine and capricious decree from which there is no escape. This leads to a fatalism in which there is no concept of sin or hope, and injustice and social decay are stoically accepted. This determinism combined with legalism is a crippling paradox for Muslims. As hard as they try to follow the rules, this belief in fate robs their hope that they could succeed and confirms their inability to be holy.

What a contrast with life in Christ! Paul wrote that, "The righteous shall live by faith." [14] Faith in the Christian life is utter dependence on God for our salvation. Muslims trust that Allah will make the decision, but we trust that God will save us. Our faith in God's faithfulness sustains us on a daily basis. Although there is a strong emphasis in Christianity on spiritual disciplines, they are not laws or rules performed to gain merit for salvation. Rather they are evidence of our faith and a natural outcome of the presence of the Holy Spirit in our lives.

Religious devotion is impressive in the eyes of men but not God. God looks at the heart, not at the words, posture, and form of our religious practices. In the same way, our success in missions is not based on methods or practices, but on faith in God, who draws [15] and enables.

---

[14] Galatians 3:11.

[15] John 6:44.

Chapter 5
Spiritual Factors

Why would a Muslim leave his family traditions, risking persecution and possibly death, in order to become a Christian? By the same token, why would a Christian convert to Islam?

Conversion is a complex phenomenon. Psychologists have studied the process, interviewed converts, and written numerous books on the factors that cause someone to leave one religion for another. Some converts are rebels who defy their family traditions by going in the opposite direction. Others are bored with their own traditions and need something new and different. Some have a genuine spiritual conversion, while others do it for more earthly reasons. I know a journalist who was not allowed to travel to Mecca to write a story on the *Kaaba*. His only option was to convert to Islam, and he did so to get the story. He told me, "It was a white lie."

On the mission field it is difficult to discern if people are genuine in their new faith or whether they convert to Christianity to obtain benefits such as jobs, humanitarian help, a visa to the USA, marriage to a Christian, or even just special attention and friendship. Christians have often been accused of exploiting weak people and converting them by financial enticements. In fairness to the missionaries, the true needs and motives of those they minister to are sometimes complex, or even guarded.

This is not unique to Christian missions. There are those who convert to Islam for similar benefits. In Egypt, Copts live under so much pressure from their Muslim neighbors and persecution by Islamic groups that they find themselves converting for safety and convenience. Some will not be promoted in their jobs unless they convert. Some convert to Islam in order to be able to divorce and remarry more easily.

The apostle Paul was well aware that false motives and methods creep into the body of Christ. He refused to play the game, writing, "We have renounced secret and shameful ways; we do not use deception, nor do we distort the word of God. On the contrary, by setting forth the truth plainly we commend ourselves to every man's conscience in the sight of God."[1] The Gospel is about what is true, and untruth can never advance it. It is not the kind of truth that comes from human wisdom and knowledge, arguments, methods, or eloquence of speech.[2] It is divine truth that is revealed directly into the hearts of men and women who have been held captives to its untruthful enemy. Paul continues, "The god of this age has blinded the minds of unbelievers, so that they cannot see the light of the Gospel of the glory of Christ, who is the image of God."

Paul learned this on the day he was blinded by the light of Jesus, who told him, "I am sending you to them to open their eyes and turn them from darkness to light, and from the power of Satan to God, so that they may receive forgiveness of sins and a place among those who are sanctified by faith in me."[3] The true Gospel is spoken into dark hearts by the Spirit of God. Though we have a role to play, genuine conversion is never possible without the Spirit of God.

What do we desire to see when we engage Muslims? I am certainly not interested in increasing the number of nominal

---

[1] 2 Corinthians 4:2, 4.

[2] I encourage the reader to take time to look up these verses that address this critical issue: 1 Corinthians 1:17; 1 Corinthians 2:2; 1 Corinthians 2:13; 1 Corinthians 2:1; 1 Thessalonians 1:5; Titus 3:9; 2 Timothy 2:23.

[3] Acts 26:18.

Christians in the world. Nor am I interested in westernizing Muslims, or in tearing down Islamic culture or Muslim countries for the sake of advancing a political or cultural agenda. Christ's "kingdom is not of this world."[4] I engage Muslims to see Christ formed inside my friends, people that I grew up among and love deeply. As Christians, our role in evangelism is to be midwives, facilitating the births of new creations in Christ. Paul put it this way when addressing the church in Galatia: "My dear children, for whom I am again in the pains of childbirth until Christ is formed in you..."[5] But when Christ is truly formed in a Muslim, it is a spiritual miracle that often has earthly repercussions.

I know many who have come out of Islam and are now servants of Christ that did not convert to Christianity in order to benefit socially, economically, or in any other earthly way. Some of them have suffered a great deal for their faith.

Why would Hisham from Kuwait give up a lucrative career, millions of dollars, suffer shame and persecution, lose contact with his family and friends and end up in exile for the sake of Christ?

What motivated Amina from Somalia to lose her family and country and face death threats for the sake of knowing Christ?

Femi was a son of the *Hojja*[6] in his mountain village in Kosova.[7] He had never met any Christians and had no understanding of Christianity or of Christ. As a college student he

---

[4] John 18:36.

[5] Galatians 4:19.

[6] *Hojja* is a religious designation for a man who does the call to prayer. In Arab countries they call him a *Muazzin*.

[7] "Kosova" is the Albanian spelling of the country, whereas "Kosovo" is the Serbian spelling.

noticed that his father was always proud of him when he came home sharing his new knowledge of science, literature, and philosophy. His father did not seem bothered by Femi quoting Gandhi or Buddha or Confucius. Then, all of a sudden when Femi mentioned that he had been reading the Bible, all hell broke loose. His father threatened to disown him if he continued on this path. Shocked, Femi reflected on this and deep down in his heart he began to gain insight into the spiritual nature of his new-found faith. This was a big part of his attraction to Jesus: it was real. His conversion was taking place in the realm of the Spirit, not through attraction to a worldly religion.

When Ibrahim, also from Kosova, first heard about Jesus from his uncle he was very angry. He could not understand why his uncle would leave the glories of Islam and follow a false religion. From his childhood, Ibrahim had been taught that Islam was the only true religion. Due to his grandfather's influence he learned all of the prayers and rituals before most of the kids his age. Now in his early twenties, the thought of his uncle leaving the true religion was repulsive to him. He and his cousin, who was his roommate, spent months arguing and debating with their uncle, desperately trying to prove the Bible wrong. Nevertheless, his cousin came to Christ during this time, and Ibrahim began having dreams in which he would accept Christ. He would wake up terrified that it might actually come true. It was not until Jesus appeared to him in a vision[8] that he began to see that Christ was freeing him from spiritual oppression.

---

[8] He experienced this vision while wide awake, reading a book about Jesus that his cousin had given him. His full testimony can be read at:
http://answering-islam.org/testimonies/ibrahim_kosovo.html.

Many who were hardened by Satan have been softened by Christ himself. Dreams and visions [9] have become a major factor in Muslims coming to know Jesus as their Lord. God still works today as he has done in the days of Joseph, Daniel and Paul, when these and many others had supernatural visitations by angels and even Christ himself.

I will never forget one Iraqi woman who came to the USA as a refugee. She had never read the Bible or understood what Christians believe. She did not need to: she was a Muslim and that settled the topic in her mind. Someone invited her to the Christmas celebration at the Arabic church that Horizons International helped start in Denver. On any other day she would have refused the invitation without blinking. But that day was different. In the middle of the day she had lain down on the couch to rest her body. She was awake, alone, and everything was quiet when she heard someone speak directly into her right ear. She told me later that if anyone would have told her those words she would have "punched him in the nose!" But these were not ordinary words, and no one was around to have said them. She had never heard anything like it ever before. As she lay there she held her breath so she wouldn't miss a word. It was clear to her without a doubt that these were not the words of a human being: "God suffered and died for you."

She told me this story in the presence of a number of others, including a convert from Egypt, and with a puzzled face she asked, "Why did God tell me these words? Why me? Why now?"

Walid was quick to answer her. "Because, as you said, if he did not tell you those words, you would not have come today to celebrate the reason for the season." He went on to explain

---

[9] Both dreams and visions are common in the testimonies of Christians from a Muslim background. The difference is that visions occur when conscious, whereas dreams occur during sleep.

that the deity of Christ is not a believable concept within a Muslim worldview.

The woman listened to these explanations. But if she hadn't had the vision, she would not have been open to the conversation in the first place. Because the Lord spoke first to her, she was now ready to hear from his followers that Jesus was born to die to save her from sin and give her new life in him. No human could have persuaded this woman against all the convictions she grew up with. No argument, no matter how clever, can persuade any Muslim that God came down in the body of Christ to die and give us life. This was the work of the Holy Spirit.

How did Peter recognize the deity of Christ and that Jesus was indeed the promised Messiah? He experienced a special revelation from above when he declared to Jesus, "You are the Messiah, son of the Living God." [10] The key to understanding the secret to the amazing truth of Peter's words is found in Jesus' response: "Blessed are you, Simon son of Jonah, for this was not revealed to you by man, but by my Father in heaven." The scriptures are clear that "no one who is speaking by the Spirit of God says, 'Jesus be cursed,' and no one can say, 'Jesus is Lord,' except by the Holy Spirit." [11]

A few months ago a Saudi student came to me, troubled by the issue of the Trinity/sonship/deity of Christ. He had rejected Islam and was searching. When he entered a church he had heard Jesus referred to as "Lord." That puzzled him. Someone told him about me so he drove fifty miles to meet me, looking for answers. I spared no argument as I shared with him. Using analogies, illustrations, and logic I explained how in nature we have many examples of trinities. Many Christians use the analogies of the triangle, the egg, the three

---

[10] Matthew 16:16.

[11] 1 Corinthians 12:3.

forms of water. My favorite is the analogy of the sun, which is comprised of fire, light, and heat. For hours I desperately tried to "prove" the deity of Christ and explain the Trinity. When he left, my hope was that he would have been convinced by something I shared with him.

Every Friday, at the end of his week's classes, Faysal again made the fifty-mile journey to see me. For the first three weeks he was stuck, unable to clear his intellectual hurdles and cultural inhibitions. We talked about many things. We read parts of the gospels and other scriptures together. This young Saudi student found Jesus very attractive. He compared Jesus with the prophet of Islam and discovered that the two leaders were as different as night and day. Yet he kept returning to the issue which was puzzling him the most. He sincerely confessed, "I am stuck."

I agonized, knowing that he would be returning to see me the next week. I so badly wanted to help him satisfy his hunger for truth. I resorted to prayer. As I prayed for Faysal that week, the Lord revealed to me that I needed to practice what I often preach. This chapter is my attempt to explain the core of what I have learned about engaging Muslims.

The apostle Paul understood this problem all too well. Although he was highly educated (he was a disciple of the famous rabbi, Gamaliel [12]) and excelled among the Jewish leaders in his knowledge and zeal, and even though he did not lack wisdom and skill in speaking, he deliberately chose not to rely on all these things in his preaching of the Gospel.

He wrote, "When I came to you, brothers, I did not come with eloquence or superior wisdom as I proclaimed to you the testimony about God. For I resolved to know nothing while I was with you except Jesus Christ and him crucified. I came to you in weakness and fear, and with much trembling. My message and my preaching were not with wise and persuasive

---

[12] Acts 22:3.

words, but with a demonstration of the Spirit's power, so that your faith might not rest on men's wisdom, but on God's power."[13]

On Faysal's fourth visit our relationship took a dramatic turn. This time I was spiritually prepared. I had failed as an "expert" who has explained the Gospel to Muslims hundreds of times and taught large gatherings of Muslims around the world. The huge library of reference materials and scholarly books that fill my office walls became useless in the face of a spiritual battle within the heart and mind of Faysal. Indeed as Paul asserted, "The weapons we fight with are not the weapons of the world. On the contrary, they have divine power to demolish strongholds."[14]

There is a battle raging within all human beings, whether they are Muslims, Christians, or atheists. It is a battle for the hearts and minds of all humans who have been subjected to sin and its power to corrupt, deafen, and blind.

Faysal was more than ready to hear about the spiritual battle for his soul. "This is not about what you *think* or *believe*," I assured him. "It is not about changing your religion. It is about your *soul*, held captive to the prince of darkness who is the enemy of God and the enemy of your soul."

When I invited him to pray and ask God to reveal himself to him he did not hesitate. After we prayed together he was ready to move on, and we have never had to discuss the Trinity again (at least we haven't yet in our relationship). Our conversations began to focus on his struggle to grasp the sacrificial love of God and Christ's work of redemption. God answered the prayer of a genuine seeker.

At its core, engaging Muslims is a *spiritual* endeavor, not an intellectual or cultural one. The battle must be won in the spiritual realm before a Muslim is able to see and hear the

---

[13] 1 Corinthians 2:1-5.

[14] 2 Corinthians 10:4.

truth. Only then will he or she be able to respond in the spirit because, "The man without the Spirit does not accept the things that come from the Spirit of God, for they are foolishness to him, and he cannot understand them, because they are spiritually discerned." [15]

So how can you apply this as you engage Muslims? What must you do when it seems that your Muslim friend is not able to accept the Gospel? First, you must remember that Jesus warned us that "...many are invited, but few are chosen." [16] Not everyone is going to receive the Good News.

I learned this lesson the hard way years ago when a Saudi student came to me with some religious questions. From the outset it was clear that he only wanted to argue. I tolerated his long, frequent, and contentious visits. Tens of hours of precious time was wasted in futile arguments over the intellectual differences between our religions. Still, my desire to see a breakthrough with him kept me motivated to persevere. As I was seeking the Lord on this student's behalf, I sensed that the Lord was not pleased with me wasting so much time. The Lord brought to my mind the words of Jesus to his disciples, "If anyone will not welcome you or listen to your words, shake the dust off your feet..." [17] It was time to end our sessions, and pray that God would soften this student's heart and open another door for him to hear the Gospel. From that experience, more than twenty years ago, I learned to look for signs of openness, and I began to seek the discernment of the Spirit regarding who to focus on.

The Bible is filled with stories demonstrating that the Lord's Kingdom is not built by might or power, but by the

---

[15] 1 Corinthians 2:14.

[16] Matthew 22:14.

[17] Matthew 10:14.

Spirit of God.[18] When David conquered the giant, was it his skill with the slingshot that did the trick?[19] Did the walls of Jericho in Joshua's days collapse because of the sound of the trumpets and the shouts of the priests?[20] What about Gideon? How could he have won with a fledgling army of only three hundred men carrying trumpets, jars, and torches?[21] Was it the praise choir at the head of Jehoshaphat's men that gave God's people victory over the vast army that was advancing against them?[22]

These stories are in the Bible to embolden us and give us reason for our faith in God's power to do what seems impossible for us as human beings. All of the men and women of God who did mighty things for God felt inadequate, yet it is that inadequacy that opened the door for God to intervene and accomplish the impossible for his glory. Thus the adage, "Man's extremity is God's opportunity."

Engaging Muslims requires the power of the Spirit to work through us. Jesus assured the disciples that, "You will receive power when the Holy Spirit comes on you and you will be my witnesses."[23] The role of the Holy Spirit is to "convict the world about sin, righteousness, and judgment..."[24] But he does that through us, "as if he were making his appeal through us."[25]

---

[18] Zechariah 4:6.

[19] I Samuel 17:45-57.

[20] Joshua 6:1-16.

[21] Judges 7:16-21.

[22] 2 Chronicles 20:1-4, 14-17, 20-23.

[23] Acts 1:8.

[24] John 16:8.

[25] 2 Corinthians 5:20.

In over forty years of ministry among Muslims I have seen many converts come and go. Some get a great start and share their testimonies boldly, but down the road they fall away. I have agonized over this problem, but I have also come to realize that some experience only an intellectual or religious–but not a spiritual–conversion.

I have learned, when speaking to individuals or groups of Muslims, to see them the way that Paul saw them: some are perishing while others are being saved. [26] A Muslim intellectual from Egypt once told me that, "It is stupid to think that a man who died two thousand years ago can do anything for me now." I live in Boulder, Colorado, and many people in my liberal city sometimes get angry when you speak to them about Jesus. One woman was quite intrigued by the music that a worship team from our church was playing on the outdoor mall downtown. When I gave her a card with our church information, her face changed and she violently returned the card to me and walked away without a word. Indeed, those who are perishing are offended by the Gospel, or they find it to be silly or foolish. But "to us who are being saved it is the power of God," [27] and Muslims whose hearts are being softened by the Holy Spirit find it powerful enough to save them. This power is available to us and is at work in us and through us as we are faithful to pray, fast, and preach the Gospel.

When I began my work with Muslims I expected resistance, arguments, and even fights. By nature and upbringing I enjoy arguing. For years, I hunted for debates with Jehovah's Witnesses, intent to prove them wrong. I collected a list of their false teachings and sharpened my intellectual weapons to defeat them. I remember several conversations that ended up as nothing but shouting matches. I got so frustrated that

---

[26] 1 Corinthians 1:17-22, 2 Corinthians 2:14-16, 2 Corinthians 4:3, 2 Thessalonians 2:10.

[27] 1 Corinthians 1:18.

out of anger I would point to them and with a loud voice I rebuked the demons inside them.

To my great disappointment this type of ministry did not yield any fruit. I finally gave it up. The Lord put me through this failure to teach me a lesson that I would never forget: "No one can come to [Jesus] unless the Father who sent [him] draws him." [28]

Even Jesus, as the master preacher of the Gospel of the Kingdom, knew that only those who are prepared for the Kingdom would follow him. This realization has set my heart at ease. It is not by human effort but by conviction of the Holy Spirit.

My friend Mehdi Dibaj was so convicted by the Holy Spirit that he could not renounce his witness of Christ, even though it cost him dearly. Why would he be willing to lose his wife, his four children, and all the pleasures of this world and *choose* to stay in jail for eleven years, if not for the sake of Christ? In a dark Iranian prison, Mehdi spent the last three years of his life in solitary confinement. He faced the judge with courage and boldness and refused to deny Christ despite the threat of a death sentence. In 1994, this modern martyr was killed after remaining faithful to the last breath. He and many others had nothing to gain from their conversion except what Christ has promised: eternal life. His conversion was of the Spirit. He joined the cloud of witnesses who "faced jeers and flogging, while still others were chained and put in prison. They were stoned; they were sawed in two; they were put to death by the sword. They went about in sheepskins and goatskins, destitute, persecuted and mistreated–the world was not worthy of them. They wandered in deserts and mountains, and in caves and holes in the ground." [29]

---

[28] John 6:44, 65.

[29] Hebrews 11:36-39.

We must be prepared to live a life in the Spirit and keep our minds and hearts on things above, not on earthly things. [30] "As it is written: 'For your sake we face death all day long; we are considered as sheep to be slaughtered.' No, in all these things we are more than conquerors through him who loved us. For I am convinced that neither death nor life, neither angels nor demons, neither the present nor the future, nor any powers, neither height nor depth, nor anything else in all creation, will be able to separate us from the love of God that is in Christ Jesus our Lord." [31]

Our purpose in engaging Muslims is not to defeat a belief system, or challenge a culture, or bring down a civilization. We don't seek to sow dissension, or overturn traditions out of disrespect. No, our motive is the same as Paul's: "I have become all things to all men so that by all possible means I might save some. I do all this for the sake of the Gospel, that I may share in its blessings." [32]

---

[30] Colossians 3:1-4.

[31] Romans 8:36-39.

[32] 1 Corinthians 9:22-23.

Chapter 6
Islam and Christianity:
How Similar are They?

Qur'anic chanting was blasting from the radio of the taxi that I hired from the Cairo airport. A tiny copy of the Qur'an was hanging from the rear view mirror and a 'hand of Fatima' was slapped on the dashboard, with a huge blue eye staring at me from the center of her palm. What other signs did I need that this driver was Muslim through and through? I began to engage him in conversation about Jesus and offered him a copy of the New Testament, which he gladly took. The ride took over an hour and the entire time I was sharing the Good News with him. Consistently he was affirming me and agreeing with me. His typical reply to me on every point: "Sure, we Muslims believe that too." I tried to show him enough differences to whet his appetite, so that he'd want to know more about God's love and the promise of forgiveness and salvation through Jesus, but it was to no avail. The man was so entrenched in the cultural value of courtesy that he did not open his mind to anything different. Communication completely failed. Or so it seemed. This is a typical conversation driven partly by politeness, but mainly by ignorance.

Christendom is divided over the issue of similarities and differences between Christianity and Islam. Most Christians would agree that there are differences, but we do not all agree on how important those differences are. One camp prefers to emphasize the similarities and use them as common ground or bridges for dialogue and communication. The other camp prefers to highlight the differences, in the interest of making the truth known about the distinctions at the core of the two belief systems.

If Islam and Christianity are both similar and different, then it is important for us to be aware of both the similarities and the differences between them. Emphasizing one or the other makes the truth lopsided. It is crucial to know what those similarities and differences are and how these relate to the core belief system of each.

Islam cannot be better-comprehended by projecting our own assumptions and aspirations onto it. Although they use similar vocabulary, Christianity and Islam are founded on opposing premises. To genuinely understand the Muslim worldview we must highlight both the similarities and differences, not ignore either. To fully engage Muslims we must understand them, and to do that we must listen to them on their own terms and in their own voice, assuming only what they assume about themselves.

And yet many Christians, in a well-intentioned desire to build bridges of understanding, do project—even *impose*—a Christian worldview onto Muslim beliefs. Bridges built this way don't lead to understanding, but only to confusion and disappointment when Islam fails to live up to the expectations these Christians bring to it.

For example, in a speech about Middle Eastern politics delivered to a group of Christians and Muslims, a prominent bishop of an evangelical denomination emphasized that all of those adhering to Judaism, Christianity, and Islam must be viewed as people of God, despite what he considered some minor differences among them. This was a charming sentiment, arising from a thoroughly Western worldview rich with Enlightenment notions of the brotherhood of man. It is also a concept foreign to both Islam and biblical Christianity.

A spokesman for a large evangelical denomination in the US, who headed its Christian-Muslim Relations Department, gave a moving speech at a church in which he recited the *fatiha* (the first chapter of the Qur'an, memorized and used in prayer by all Muslims) with tears in his eyes. He made comparisons between it and the Lord's Prayer. He did admit that there may be differences but stressed that at heart they are both prayers of praise to God Most High.

After hearing a lecture by a seminary professor, a student told me, "I never knew how similar Islam and Christianity were. Now I know that all Muslims need is to be enlightened." Another well-respected speaker on Islam, who has trained dozens of Christian missionaries to the Muslim world, is convinced that Muhammad almost became a Christian and that at one time all his teachings were congruent with biblical teachings. He claims that the Qur'an is an adequate tool for leading Muslims to Christ if only we would present it with proper biblical interpretation. But one cannot take either religion seriously and assert that a veneer of "enlightenment" or a smattering of ecumenical texts can save a life that is not surrendered to its core to either Christ or Allah.

Though beautiful in expression and charitable in spirit towards Muslims, these sorts of Christian leaders imply that with some improvements–minor or major–Islam can be corrected and set onto the right path.

Is Islam really so similar to Christianity that it is hard to discern the essential differences? Or are we surrendering to a version of the old saying, "All roads lead to Rome?" Are we being squeezed into the present mold of pluralistic thinking, compromise, tolerance, and accommodation? Or do we have cold feet when it comes to confronting people living in the dark with the good news of the light of the world? [1] Samuel Zwemer, in dealing with the apparent similarities between Christianity and Islam, expressed it well: "With regret, it must be admitted that there is hardly an important fact concerning

---

[1] John 8:12, John 9:5.

the life, person and work of our Saviour which is not ignored, perverted or denied by Islam." [2]

Islam accepts Jesus as a prophet, but denies his sonship and redemptive death on the cross. Islam believes in God the creator, but denies that he is a personal, loving father. Islam accepts the books of the Bible, but claims that they are no longer reliable and that the Bible we have today has been corrupted. Islam believes that there is a hell and a heaven, but provides no way to secure the believer's destiny except *jihad*, martyrdom, or dying during the *hajj*. [3] Not to mention that the Islamic heaven is a place for eating, drinking, and orgies, not the holy dwelling place of a holy God. How can we accept Muslims as people of God if they have not believed his word and have rejected his Son? Our ministry to Muslims is ineffective and useless until we recognize the lostness of Muslims and bring to them the good news of God's love and salvation.

Taking both religions seriously means that you can follow Jesus *or* Islam. You cannot have both. As the prophet Elijah warned at Mount Carmel, "How long will you waver between two opinions? If the LORD is God, follow him; but if Baal is God, follow him." [4] Jesus made it clear that, "You cannot serve two masters." [5]

For your Muslim friend, religion is not a matter of intellectual or theological conviction. It is not a set of beliefs. It is an identity drawn from his family, society, culture, and country. If you cross the social barrier you are faced with a cultural wall. If you are able to climb that wall you may find yourself

---

[2] *The Muslim Christ*, London, 1912. Zwemer was one of the early pioneers of twentieth century evangelical missions to Arab Muslims.

[3] Many Muslims believe that dying during the *hajj* or *jihad* will guarantee entrance to heaven.

[4] 1 Kings 18:21.

[5] Luke 16:13.

trapped in a vicious circle of arguments about the Trinity and the reliability of the Bible. When you challenge your Muslim friend to consider the claims of Christ, he may not perceive that you are speaking of truth, facts, or doctrines. Instead, he will probably feel that you are questioning the totality of who he is: his family, society, culture, and country. The Muslim's unquestioning acceptance of his identity is perhaps the most serious roadblock in communicating the Gospel to him.

Terminology Differences

Every religion has a vocabulary. What does that religion mean by terms like "God," "sin," or "salvation?" How does it define "faith," "belief," "charity," or "martyrdom?" Just because two religions have similar terminology, it doesn't mean that those terms are equivalent. To actually understand a religion we must understand how it defines its own terms, not just fill them with our own meanings.

In recent years, several Bible translations have been produced using Qur'anic terminology in an effort to make the Bible more "Muslim friendly." Some bold translators have gone so far as to remove the expression "Son of God," replacing it with terms like "beloved of God" or even "Caliph of God." Christian concepts cannot adequately be carried out in Islamic forms. We cannot assume that we are communicating effectively with a Muslim by merely replacing Christian terms and idioms with Islamic words. If the Christian assumes these terms are equivalent then he and his Muslim friend will be talking past each other. Rather than crossing a bridge of understanding, they will have sunk into a mire of confusion.

Let's look at just a few simple examples of the ways Muslim and Christian worldviews differ.

God vs. Allah

When Bilquis Sheikh, a Pakistani from a Muslim noble family, learned about the fatherhood of God in the Bible, she was blown away. Her book *I Dared to Call Him Father*[6] is an amazing testimony to the intimate father-child relationship we can have through Jesus. Many Muslims are drawn by the love of the heavenly Father. Christian theology sees God as a loving Father who created man in his own image and who desires intimate fellowship with his children.

To the Muslim, God is a distant sovereign who is uninvolved with his creation, yet he dictates his predetermined demands. Those in Christ see themselves as adopted children, whereas Muslims see themselves as slaves who have no choice but to perform their preordained duties. Obedience is expected of the Christian, stemming out of a loving relationship with their heavenly Father. But Muslims are taught obedience out of fear of the judgement of an unpredictable, capricious deity.

Hasan, a Shiite Lebanese, was terrified of God's judgement. As a ten-year-old, he watched a soccer coach screaming at the players during practice. This became his picture of God. That was when he began to have nightmares about God judging him on a soccer field, never satisfied with his performance and condemning his every mistake. He was twenty-two years old when I met him and began to witness to him. He needed an answer to the question, "How can I avoid God's judgement?" His image of himself was that of a fearful slave belonging to an angry God. It took two hours to explain to Hasan that Jesus came to set him free, and that he took the penalty on himself so that we might be declared righteous. His heart was relieved and he surrendered his life to Christ.

---

[6] Bilquis Sheikh with Richard H. Shneider, *I Dared to Call Him Father*, (Grand Rapids, MI: Chosen Books, 1978,2003).

While Christians celebrate God's attributes reflecting his relational nature, Muslims utter his names by rote. Christians are instructed to not utter God's name in vain, Muslims are pressured to repeat his name constantly and many resort to prayer beads to help them do so throughout the day. Islam and Christianity both acknowledge God's transcendence, omnipotence, and majestic qualities. Yet the Muslim concept of God lacks the most distinctive qualities of his immanence, his fatherhood, his love, and his active involvement in our daily lives. While we as Christians "approach the throne of grace with confidence,"[7] a Muslim comes with fear and trembling.[8]

This difference has consequences. While Christians aspire to fellowship and intimacy with God, Muslims have no such hope–or even the expectation that such a hope is possible. To a Muslim, the idea of that sort of relationship with Allah is not only incomprehensible, it is objectionable. It would imply that Allah would lower himself to relate directly with a human, which would lessen his glory. A Christian who asks a Muslim if he has a "personal relationship" with God is asking about something that is not only impossible, but absurd. We cannot

---

[7] Hebrews 4:16.

[8] I am aware that some exceptions exist such as the Sufis, elements of Shiism, various other types of mystical Muslims, and moderate Muslims who have borrowed attractive concepts from Christianity into their Islamic identity. What I have described here is mainstream Islamic theology.

simply substitute the term "Allah" for "God" and expect to be understood. [9]

Theology and Belief System

Although you might find your Muslim friend to be brilliant in his academic field, when it comes to his religion he has a very different understanding of religious truth. Ordinary Muslims are not generally theologically-minded, although in recent decades there has been a greater awareness of doctrinal differences between Islam and Christianity. These are used in polemics and apologetics in debates. But the ordinary Muslims are works-oriented. They are trying to earn their salvation by their obedience to God's law (Sharia).

When dealing with Muslims face-to-face, we naturally imagine them to be like us, and therefore we start our "theological" exchange. But more often than not, we miss the target and end up communicating ineffectively. We therefore must understand that the Muslim is at the other end of the spectrum from the Christian when it comes to theology. Muhammad himself condemned theology and considered it the enemy of "religion" (the Muslim understanding of the term). In the commentary of his translation of the Qur'an, Muhammad (formerly Marmaduke) Pickthall, a British convert to Islam observed that, "When they [the Jews] found that they could not make use of the newcomer [Muhammad], they opposed him and tried to bewilder him with questions from their the-

---

[9] The use of Allah in Christian witness and Bible translation is a complex topic which could be the subject of another book. I cannot do justice to it here. However, it is worthwhile to mention that even though Arabic-speaking Christians have no other word but Allah, that does not automatically mean that the word Allah should be used in other languages of Muslims. For instance, Iranians from Muslim background prefer *Khoda*, the Farsi word for God, because "Allah" has strictly Islamic connotations for them.

ology, speaking to him as men who possessed superior wisdom; failing to perceive that, from a Prophet's standpoint, theology is childish nonsense, the very opposite of religion, and its enemy; religion, for the prophet, being not a matter of conjecture and speech, but of fact and conduct." [10]

This should warn us not only to avoid speaking in our own theological terms, but also to be aware that we should not use our own knowledge of Islam to pin a Muslim's beliefs down in hypothetical arguments.

In my experience and knowledge of Islam and Muslims, I have found more success in avoiding the polemical issues that only exacerbate conflict, and sticking to a straight presentation of the Gospel story. Although we should all be ready to "give answer" [11] on the doctrinal topics, I find that when you get to the issues of the heart, Muslims will go there with you.

The Bible vs. The Qur'an

For Christians, the Bible is food for the mind, heart, and soul. We read it, study it, memorize it, and meditate on it. We write in its margins, highlight words and verses, wear it out, and carry it around with us. We place it anywhere convenient: a shelf, a chair, the floor, and when it gets worn out we throw it in the trash. Nothing is holy about the physical pages; the words convey holy content. The Bible is the product of many different writers, in different languages and from different cultures, assembled over centuries. We have organizations dedicated to translating it into every language and dialect, including paraphrases so that we might better grasp its mean-

---

[10] Muhammad M. Pickthall, *The meaning of the glorious Qur'an: text and explanatory translation,* 1st ed. (Tahrike Tarsile Qur'an, 2001).

[11] 1 Peter 3:15 is commonly referenced as supporting apologetic readiness, although the verse itself refers to being prepared to give a *testimony* of "the reason for the hope that you have."

ing. The Bible is not sacred as a *book;* the Word of God that it contains and communicates is what is valuable. But Muslims have a very different understanding of–and relationship with– the Qur'an.

When Muhammad allegedly first heard the voice of an angel, he was told to "recite" what he was told. During his twenty-three year career as the prophet of Islam, the angel Gabriel allegedly continued to ask him to recite these verses. The collection of all the recitations in one volume is called the Qur'an ("The Recitation"). This means that the Qur'an is the very words of God, delivered verbatim by the angel Gabriel to Muhammad and recited to the *Umma* (the Islamic community). These words are said to have been written in heaven before the creation. When the time came for them to be revealed they were dictated to Muhammad who in turn dictated them to his companions, who memorized them and kept them until they were written down. The Qur'an is said to have been prewritten word for word, with no human element involved. [12]

Study of the Qur'an is traditionally reserved for scholars and teachers of Islam. For ordinary Muslims, especially those who do not know Arabic, the Qur'an is to be recited for its religious value, in order to gain merit with Allah. Allah is pleased with you when you read the Qur'an, and even more pleased when you memorize it and recite it by heart.

The Qur'an is in Arabic and when translated it is no longer considered the Qur'an, rather the "Meanings of the Qur'an." Therefore, the Qur'an can only be recited in Arabic. This means that all Muslims have to learn to at least pronounce Arabic so that they can pray and recite the Qur'an. Most do

---

[12] Most Muslims are unaware of textual criticism of the Qur'an, which only recently has been addressed. Those I have talked to have not even thought about the practical steps of how the Qur'an was collected or the fact that it is impossible to have a manuscript without human error.

not learn it as a language of communication, but only in order to read the Qur'an. Most Muslims who read the Qur'an in Arabic as a second language do not understand it, they just pronounce it. This is completely different than the evangelical Christian use of the Bible. I have never heard of Muslims getting together for a Wednesday night "Qur'an study," to discuss, explore, and interpret the Qur'an and apply it to their daily lives. The Qur'an is not taught to be understood by the masses. It's taught to be recited for gaining merit with God. The Sharia, not the Qur'an, is what dictates the daily life of a Muslim.

There are various *hadiths* showing how different famous Muslim leaders have read the entire Qur'an every three days or every week or every month or every forty days. One *hadith* sets the minimum to ten verses a day. The whole point is to recite it, not to understand it. Reading it, whether it is understood or not, conveys righteousness and blessing. During Ramadan, Muslims are expected to read the entire Qur'an at least once. Some scholars recommend that the Qur'an should be read all night during waking hours. Once, my wife and I were riding in a taxi in Egypt with our son and his family when the baby began to cry. The radio in the taxi was tuned to a station broadcasting a continual reading (chanting) of the Qur'an. We asked the driver to shut off the radio to allow the baby to sleep. He said he cannot do that because he did not want to break the chain of having the Qur'an read non-stop during his work hours.

Muslims have a very different understanding of the world, perspective on life, and belief system than Christians. Ignoring those differences by dwelling on commonalities does not truly allow us to understand their beliefs, or help us articulate our response to them. Instead, it perpetuates misunderstandings and obscures the distinctions that are so necessary to effectively reach Muslims. We must avoid conceit: what *we want to believe* about Muslims is not more important than what *they believe* about themselves. To engage Muslims we must engage them based on the truth regarding who they are, what they really believe, and how they live out their religion. That includes not only hard facts, (where they live, what language they speak, practical details of their culture and lifestyle, etc.), but also the intangibles that make up their worldview. In the next chapter we will look at how the Arab origins of Islam have shaped the Muslim worldview.

Chapter 7
The Arab Character of Islam

Not all Muslims are Arabs. As we pointed out earlier, only twenty percent of the world's one billion-plus Muslims are. In spite of this, Islam is essentially an Arab religion. Not only did its vocabulary, character, and worldview arise from the Arab culture of Muhammad's day, but it holds to Arab culture as an ideal to which Muslims should aspire. Therefore, to understand even non-Arab Muslims we must take a look at the character and worldview of the Arabs.

Arab Character

The worldview that was captured in the Qur'an and *Hadith* was shaped by and reflects the desert life of the Arabs. This harsh and unrelenting environment shapes the very character of the Arab as surely as it carves its ever-changing, wind-swept mountains of sand. If environment drives the history and character of a people, then surely the Arabs were shaped by the desert every bit as much as the dunes. Let's consider some of those characteristics.

Pessimism: The hardship of desert life, the lack of color and variety in the environment, the traditional belief in fate (*qadaa' wa qadar*), and their concept of God as a distant, arbitrary dictator cast a pessimistic shadow in the Arab mind. Their music is often sad, dwelling on lost friends and lovers and regrets over unsuccessful relationships. This pessimism also causes the Arab to surrender to hardships unquestionably as if his portion (*nasib*) in life leaves him no choices.

Resistance to Authority: Unlike their neighbors in Persia, Turkey, and Ethiopia, the Arabs had no king or ruler to unite them and look after their common interests. No single tribe was ever able to gain authority or leadership over the others. Even Muhammad's tribe, the Quraish, were not perceived by the Arabs as the leading tribe although they held a prominent position as keepers of the *Kaaba*, the holy temple of all the Arab tribes. The famous independent streak of the Arabs is derived from their unsettled and restless origins. Arabs do not respect authority and cannot successfully handle a democratic system. Ibn Khaldun (1332-1406 AD), the famous Arab historian, philosopher, and sociologist observed, "Arabs are resistant to one another's leadership and control. Even the tribal chiefs had little authority over their people." [1] Totalitarian regimes from within and without have been the only means of controlling the Arabs. Resistance to authority is largely responsible for the political unrest which has persisted throughout the centuries in Arab lands.

Carelessness and Lack of Organization: Ibn Khaldun also observed that Arab homes and cities were haphazardly built and poorly maintained. This characteristic may have its roots in the traditions of constant mobility in Arab culture. They tended to not settle down long enough in any one place to organize themselves. Although things are changing since the Arabs have begun using Western systems and technology, their disorderly character is still evident on various personal and social levels. A prime example is the manner in which Arabs in general fail (or refuse) to obey traffic rules or drive in lanes clearly marked on the main streets. This does not mean that all Arabs are this way. There are Arabs who are highly organized, but they tend to be ones who have experienced Western influence through education, travel, or business.

Time: Time is strictly measured in the West. Americans tend to monitor their day by the minute, while Arabs think of

---

[1] *Introduction to History* Ibn Khaldun. Al Muqaddima. In Arabic. No known English edition.

the day as loose blocks of time. Bear this in mind when your dinner guest shows up an hour or more late. An Arabic "five minutes" is usually no less than fifteen to twenty-five minutes by the clock. In Lebanese Arabic, when one says "tomorrow" (*bukra*), it can, depending on the context, refer to an indistinct time in the near future, days or even months later. One must say *"bukra bukra"* or *"bukra ssubu7"* [2] (tomorrow morning) to actually indicate one calendar day in the future.

Temper: In his book on eloquence and its expression, Al Jahiz (a famous Arab scholar of the ninth century), described the Arab as "temperamental, easily provoked to anger for the meanest reason, ready to kill if his honor has been hurt." [3] The Arab temperament is not much different today. You see this in the streets, marketplace, and movie theaters, where it is common for people to pick a fight over almost anything. Yet Arabs can also be quite humorous and easy-going. Just as quickly as their tempers flare up, they will often almost instantly turn from yelling to joking, smiling, and shaking hands.

Traditions: The Arab is a conformist when it comes to his traditions and values such as hospitality, honor, friendship, courage, and pride. These values are protected by a complex system embedded in the family, clan, and the larger social group.

Courage: Due to the struggle for survival and constant invasions and looting of other tribes, the Arabs had to develop courage and might. Acts of courage are hailed greatly, while cowardice is condemned by family, friends, and the society. A typical Arab is more inclined to die than risk being called a

---

[2] The number "7" is commonly used in the Arab world to represent the Arabic letter "Ha" (ح, hard "H" sound) in Latin script. I have chosen to include it in certain instances, to aid Arabic learners in correct pronunciation.

[3] Al Jahiz, *"Kitab al-Bayan wa al-Tabyin"* (*The Book of eloquence and exposition*), (undated) in Arabic, my translation.

coward. Perhaps this partly explains the suicidal tendencies of Arab terrorists.

Loyalty: If you succeed in becoming a friend to an Arab you will be his friend forever. In my childhood, when it appeared that I had found a true friend, he and I would poke little holes in our index fingers. We would mingle our blood as a sign that we would be loyal to one another forever. Blood is a symbol of loyalty, as demonstrated by proverbs such as "blood never becomes water," which means that once we are related by blood we will be loyal to death.

Honor and Pride (*al3ard wal sharaf*): Preservation of personal honor–and that of the family, tribe, and country–is one of the Arabs' primary values. It is unwise to be critical of any Arab with whom you deal. Arabs are extremely sensitive to what you think of them. They are not open to constructive criticism. Arab life is controlled by this value in all aspects—social, political, and others. Arabs flatter each other face-to-face even when much animosity exists underneath. This value is passionately defended when it comes to the reputation (*al3ard*) of women. If a woman gets a reputation for immorality, even if she is only suspected of immoral conduct, she may be killed by her brothers or her father in order to preserve the reputation of the family. Honor killings are quite common in many Arab countries even today.

Revenge (*intiqaam*): Revenge is a natural outcome of the Arab concept of honor. Arab literature is obsessed with stories of revenge. A typical plot in these stories involves a son growing to adulthood only to discover that his father, older brother, or an uncle was murdered years before. He will not rest until he finds the culprit and takes revenge. The family, clan, and tribe will shame him and ostracize him if he fails to fulfill his duty to avenge their honor. Arabs had elaborate codes regarding revenge which are still practiced in various forms. Vengeance does not seem to stop at any point, but continues for generations. It is not within the scope of this book to explore this topic, but I would only mention that the

Sunni-Shiite struggle is, to a large extent, rooted in the spirit of avenging the murder of Ali's son Hussein by the Sunni rivals for the Caliphate.

Hospitality (*diaafa*): Perhaps the most representative quality of the Arabs is their lavish hospitality. Arabs will sacrifice time, money, comfort, and almost anything else to show hospitality. A poor family will borrow money or sell a precious piece of property in order to spread a large banquet for a guest. An extreme example of hospitality comes from the eighth century: a Bedouin family, having failed to find game to hunt in the desert, resorted to slaying their baby to feed a passing guest. Hospitality is the key to the Arab's heart. The owner of a gas station in Lebanon recently invited me and four of my family members to lunch just because I got out of my car to greet him in his office and ask him for directions. He could not get himself to just give me directions without expressing some sort of hospitality. When I resisted his repeated invitation, he reached out to his closet and opened a case of chocolate candy and offered us a handful.

Romance (*alghazal*): Arab literature and poetry is romantic. Themes include the desert, the home, women, camels, nature, and high ideals. Al Jahiz saw the Arab as intelligent, but not creative. His words may be beautiful but they are hollow, and void of meaning. Arab education instills in Arab youth an infatuation with romance and idealism even at the expense of realism. The Arab is not down-to-earth, but rather is immersed in a world of intuition, feelings, ambitions, and aspirations. This is clearly seen in literature, film, and in personal correspondence among relatives and friends.

Intuition: Ahmad Amin, a contemporary Egyptian writer, notes that the Arab does not think logically but rather intuitively and spontaneously. [4] He tells stories of Arab superstition

---

[4] Ahmad Amin, *Fajr Al Islam* (The Dawn of Islam), (Cairo: Nahda Press 1982), in Arabic.

and legends that have no logical basis, and claims that this characteristic is deeply rooted in the Arab character. As an example, he points out that Arab poetry is so illogical and disjointed that you can shuffle the lines in any order and no one would notice unless he was familiar with the original sequence. The same is true of most works of Arabic literature which, although they may contain great ideas and interesting information, do not follow a logical sequence and have no coherence or unifying theme. They are collections of thoughts and facts put together spontaneously. The Qur'an is a prime example of this—most verses express disconnected ideas that have no cohesiveness or continuity with the surrounding verses. In fact, you can observe that rhyme takes precedence over intelligibility. Words and phrases are thrown together because they sound good. For example, biblical names are changed in the Qur'an to fit the rhyme. Cain and Abel (*qayin wa habil*) of the Bible are Cable and Abel (*qabil wa habil*) in the Qur'an. While Arab Christians call Jesus *Yasou3*, the Qur'an calls him *Isa* (*3isa*), perhaps in order to rhyme with *Musa* (Moses). Such transformation of words is allowable in the rules of Arabic poetry and is quite common. Beauty of expression is often a higher value than truth.

The Arab-Muslim Identity: Arabs take pride in the fact that–as they believe–God has chosen them, to the exclusion of all others, to receive his final and most complete revelation. They claim that other revelations, including that of Jesus, were relevant only for certain nations, in their language, and for their time. They say that since the language of their revelation is in Arabic, which they allege is the language of Adam and of God, it is the language of Islam. So, strictly speaking, "anyone who becomes a Muslim becomes an Arab."[5] Islam as a religion and Arabism as a national identity are inseparable

---

5 Al-Hariri, p. 23, quoted from Abdul Aziz Al-Duri in his book Arab Nationalism and Islam, p. 67, in Arabic.

according to Arab-Muslim thinkers. Muhammad 'Ammara is one of many who has declared proudly that, "Islam as a religion, despite its being international and superseding the limits of culture, ethnicity and nationalism, requires of all its followers...to become Arab."⁶ On many occasions, Arab leaders have expressed the indisputable formula that, "A Muslim is an Arab, an Arab is a Muslim." Lebanese scholar Philip Hitti states unequivocally that, "As Persians, Syrians, Copts, Berbers, and others flocked to the fold of Islam, the nationality of the Muslim receded into the background. No matter what his nationality may have been originally, the follower of Muhammad now passed for an Arab."⁷ The Qur'an supports this mentality, assuring that, "You are the best nation that has been brought to mankind."⁸ Muslim scholars have understood this verse to be addressed to both Arabs and Muslims.

This perspective causes an identity crisis for most Muslims with other ethnic identities. For instance, it would be hard for an Indonesian to think of himself as an Arab even though he thinks Arabic is a divine language. Most non-Arab Muslims suffer from a sort of inferiority complex caused by this idealized view of Arab language and heritage.

Proverbs and Wisdom: When my sister talks to me on the phone I often grab a pen and paper to write down any new proverb that I have not yet heard, to add to the hundreds of proverbs I have learned since my childhood. It would be rare for any two Arabs to speak with each other without using proverbs. There is power to this style of speaking. If you can find a proverb to support your point, you basically win the argument. Arabic literature and poetry is filled with both ancient and current proverbs. Some proverbs are made up on the

⁶ Ammara, Muhammad, *Islam and Arabism*, (Beirut: Dar al Wihda, 1981), in Arabic.

⁷ Philip K Hitti, *The Arabs*, (London: Mcmillan & Co. Ltd, 1950).

⁸ Qur'an, Sura 3:110.

spot. "As the proverb goes..." is usually how it begins. It is important to remember that Arabs are not necessarily persuaded by logic, but by the wisdom of the ancients. The credibility of poet so and so, king such and such, or this or that author carries much weight in the minds of Arabs.

Humor: Arabs, especially Egyptians, constantly joke about each other and themselves. On a recent visit to Egypt, an Egyptian man told me this joke: three men–an American, a Japanese, and an Egyptian–met in hell. They asked the guard to let them call home to warn their families not to end up in this horrible place. When they were done they lined up to pay. The American was charged $1,000. The Japanese paid only $100. But when the Egyptian man came to pay, the guard said, "For you, it is free." Surprised, the Egyptian asked the reason for this unexpected generosity. The guard grunted, "From hell to hell is a local call. Go away."

Superstition and Folk Religion: Pre-Islamic Arabia was predominantly animistic. They believed that spirits are present in all inanimate objects and that they have power in their lives. I grew up believing that I was born with my own personal evil spirit double, the *qarina*. Although I was a Christian, this belief infected me through the predominant culture of Islam where I grew up. The *qarina* is your familiar spirit that haunts you all your life and fills your heart with fear of the evil eye. This belief has filled the heart of every Arab with fear from before the advent of Islam to now. The Arabs have always been extremely superstitious.

Unity: The Unfulfilled Dream of the Arabs

Unity has been the heart's desire of all the Arabs since before the arrival of Islam. A prominent Muslim leader said in a speech directed to an American ambassador: "We look at all Arab nations...as one country." [9] From the beginning of his

---

[9] Abdul Aziz Al Douri, *Islam and Arab Nationalism*, p. 67. In Arabic.

career, Muhammad was obsessed with unifying the feuding Arab tribes with their three-hundred-sixty rival gods. However, the term "Arab" does not identify a homogeneous ethnic people. There has never been a country or a people whose only identity was Arab. Arabs have always been something else, *plus* Arab.

In the early twentieth century various movements, clubs, publications, and political parties dedicated to the cause of unity were launched in various Arab countries. Perhaps the only attempt that has lasted to the present is the Arab League, founded in 1945 along the lines of the United Nations. But the function of the Arab League has been quite limited for many reasons, mainly because it is being used by the various political regimes as a platform for their ideologies and attacks on their opponents.

At the Arab League meeting held in Damascus in 2008, the Libyan dictator Moammar Qaddafi caused a backlash when he scolded Arab leaders for their disunity. He harshly accused Arab rulers for seeking their own interest rather than a common Arab cause.

Arab unity has not been possible, despite the many attempts. Those who promote unity tend to be idealistic and philosophical rather than realistic. They overlook the many obstacles to unity such as ethnic diversity and the Sunni-Shiite struggle.

The Islamic world has a volatile nature, which the Israeli-Palestinian conflict has only exacerbated. Arab countries have been struggling for centuries to find their distinct identities and affirm their independence. Colonial powers forced Arab nations to run to the East to communist powers, who armed them to the hilt. As they prepared themselves in unison to "push Israel into the sea" they found themselves preempted by an Israeli attack that paralyzed their military might in the Six-Day War of 1967. Their ally, the Soviet Union, did not come to their rescue.

Disappointed and shamed by the worst defeat in their history, Arab leaders blamed all their ills on the East and the West. Voices of reform called for a severance of ties with both world powers and Islam was promoted as the third alternative. "Islam is the Answer," became a common slogan. This is when Khomeini returned from exile in 1979 to topple the Kingdom of Persia (Iran). Muslims were ready to give Islam a chance.

Many countries began to call for an Islamic uprising against the secular governments. Attempts to impose Islamic Sharia were spearheaded by militant Islamists throughout the Arab world. All have failed.

Seeing that Islam did not deliver on the promises of uniting the Arabs, Muslim people began to feel helpless and hopeless against the great powers. An identity crisis emerged and continues to the present. The reaction to this crisis varies from those who try harder by becoming more fundamentalist to those who have turned their hearts toward secularism with its material incentives.

Now, more than three decades after the Khomeini revolution, the Muslim world is still in flux. Moderates have to decide between extremism and liberalism. The tug of war continues.

The cultural values of "saving face" and never confronting your "Arab brother" directly makes it almost impossible to confront real issues. The Arabs are plagued with mistrust and deception. Islamization has often been a divisive, rather than a unifying factor. Dishonesty lies behind much of the outward code of etiquette. In fact, Arab leaders, while rendering graceful compliments to each other, have spent fortunes in plotting each other's assassinations. Each Arab country is at war not only with its neighbors, but with itself as well. Each wants to prosper and advance the way the West has, yet each is attached to its cultural, ethnic, and religious traditions and wants to revert to the past. This conflict is experienced by the man on the street as much as by the top political and religious leaders. There is no doubt that all Islamic countries agree in principle that they should all belong to one Islamic nation. Yet the questions of how this unity would be achieved, under whose regime it would be governed, and which religious sect it would follow, continue to plague their relationships.

Political unity has been the dream and aspiration of many–not only Muslim nations. No people, nation, or group of nations enjoys disunity. The United Nations is supposed to bring the world together in unity and avoid conflicts. The premise is that if only people would shake hands with each other, if only they would sit around the same table and dialogue, then they could resolve their differences in a spirit of sincerity, honesty, cooperation, mutual interests, peace, unity, etc.

To me, these sound like the sentiments that built the tower of Babel. And yet this desire for unity is something that God has planted in our hearts, something we inherited from his very nature. The problem arises when we look to mankind to unify itself. No political or religious system can solve the core problem with the world: man's rebellion against God. True unity is only achievable by the work of God in our hearts. Humans do not need to be *reformed*, they need to be *transformed*.

As servants of the Gospel we have opportunities that we never had before. There is a gap, a void that must be filled. The global Church needs to learn how to satiate the spiritual hunger of Muslims. This must be done by communicating the Gospel in ways that they understand. Understanding the Arab character helps us to clarify the Gospel when speaking to Muslims. This is very different from trying to assimilate the Gospel based on surface cultural forms. We cannot do the Gospel justice without a deep understanding of Muslim values and attitudes. But the good news is that the more we do understand their character, the more useful Christ's teachings show themselves to be.

Today, there is an unprecedented hunger in the hearts of Muslims. In this era, Muslims are choosing sides between the oppression of Islamization and the moral perils of westernization. We need to show them the way out of both of these traps. It is a proven fact that millions of Muslims are finding Jesus to be attractive because they are hungry for love, acceptance, and security. But these are only the ones who have heard Christ's message in some way. Hundreds of millions more have never had a chance to respond to the message of redemption because they have never heard it. They don't know that Jesus can give them a new identity in him, as sons and daughters of God.

Chapter 8
Muslim Identity

In 1949 I was born in a farm village near Zgharta, in the hills of northeastern Lebanon. World War II had just ended and the Middle East was undergoing a change that has shaped it ever since: the year before, the nation of Israel declared its independence in Palestine, on Lebanon's southern border. That sparked the Arab-Israeli War, which drove hundreds of thousands of Palestinian refugees into surrounding countries, mostly Jordan, Syria, Egypt, and Lebanon.

This turmoil crushed Lebanon's economy. When I was two years old my father moved our family down from the hills into the Lebanese port city of Tripoli to find work as a builder. We weren't alone: like my father, many farmers were forced to leave mountain villages and seek manual labor in the city. Poverty forced us to live in a slum on the hillside above the city. I was the youngest of four children, and the six of us shared a twelve-by-thirteen-foot room, with an outhouse and outdoor kitchen which we shared with three other families.

I was used to the sounds of a Maronite[1] mountain farm village, waking up to the enchanting crow of roosters and braying of donkeys. But once we moved to the "big city," each morning just before the break of dawn my body would be jolted from slumber by the deafening cry of the *azan*, the Muslim call to prayer. It blasted from loudspeakers directly into our window from the minaret, only a block away. Two seconds later another cry from the mosque two blocks in the

---

[1] The Maronites are a Catholic faction founded by a Hermit named Maroun in the hills of present Lebanon. They are the dominant Christian sect in Lebanon.

other direction would join in, and within five seconds the call
to prayer was blaring from five different mosques in the
neighborhood–as if one mosque was not enough to wake up
everyone in the entire city! Five shrieks overlaid on top of
each other, starting just seconds apart, sounded like a brass
band blowing the same tune but in different keys and out of
time. From my earliest memories, my daily dose of Islam began with the azan. The chant rang in my ears for a long time
and I could never get back to sleep afterward. Of course, that
was the point: the dawn call to prayer was supposed to get the
faithful of the city up and moving. The louder, the more imposing, and the more jarring the noise, the more effective the
broadcasts were in convincing sleepy people that, *"Assa-
laaaaaaatu Khayyyyyyyrun minnnnnaaaaa Nawm!"* ("Prayer is
better than sleep.") The azan is chanted slowly, each word is
sustained for several seconds and every line repeated twice.
The entire prayer takes three to five minutes:

> *God is greater,*
> *There is no god but Allah.*
> *I testify that Muhammad is the messenger of Allah*
> *Hasten to prayer, Hasten to prosperity*
> *Prayer is better than sleep*
> *God is greater*
> *There is no god but Allah.*

Muslim life is structured around the recital of set prayers
to Allah. Five times a day, every day, all around the globe at
very specific times from dawn to bedtime, hundreds of millions of ears are exposed to these haunting chants. To be fair,
Christian monks structure their lives around regular hours of
prayer as well, and Middle-Eastern churches often compete
with the mosques through the loud toll of their bells. But the
public life of even private citizens in a Muslim nation is regu-
lated around Islamic rituals. This is only one example of how
the lifestyle and worldview of Muslims is very different from

modern Westerners, who have largely banished religion from the public square and the rhythms of daily living.

We were not Muslims. Christianity had thrived in Lebanon for six hundred years before the Islamic Arab conquest in the seventh century. It again passed to Christian rule for a couple of hundred years during the Crusades. As a result, Lebanon still has a large Christian minority, to which my Greek Orthodox family belonged. Growing up as a religious minority in a predominantly Muslim city, I began to grasp the Muslim worldview through daily interactions with kids in the neighborhood. I noticed the differences between my family's lifestyle and that of our neighbors and friends. Lifestyle and practice are the keys to understanding the worldview of ordinary Muslims: Islamic prayer is only one example.

We misunderstand their perspective if we look only at Islamic theology or formal Islam. In fact, the majority of Muslims do not know or understand their own belief system from a theological perspective. Eighty percent of Muslims do not have a working knowledge of the Arabic language, in which they are required to say their prayers. And a large portion of Arabs who can speak the language are illiterate. The Qur'an is written in high, classical Arabic which is difficult to understand even for the semi-educated and some of it is completely unintelligible without interpretation. Yet its poetic verses charm its reciters, and its repetition permeates and controls Islamic society.

Christianity is focused on internal change, but Islam emphasizes external works. Whereas the Bible teaches, "Do not conform any longer to the pattern of this world, but be transformed by the renewing of your mind,"[2] the Qur'an insists that "any who believe in Allah and the Last Day, and work

---

[2] Romans 12:2.

righteousness, shall have their reward with their Lord..."[3] Islam was designed to encompass and control every aspect of life, be it religious, moral, social, cultural, economic, or political. The best way to form an accurate impression of how Muslims see the world and themselves is to observe their practices in those aspects of life.

Islamic Identity

My middle school friend, Zeinab, was as much of a Muslim as her grandmother, Fatima. There were obvious differences: the old lady dressed with a veil covering her face in public or when men were present. She also consistently practiced the "Five Pillars" of Islam. Zeinab, on the other hand, did not cover herself or pray five times a day except during Ramadan, the month of fasting. She prayed sometimes, but mostly under pressure from her grandmother and especially when guests were present. But despite the contrasts in their lifestyles, Zeinab's identity was clear; she was a Muslim.

From an early age, Muslims learn that they are Muslim simply because they were born to Muslim parents. They solidify their Islamic identity by conforming to their society, culture, and the political system under which they live. One prayer, often repeated by Muslims says, "Praise be to the Lord of the worlds for having created me a Muslim." Muslim scholars support this concept by teaching that all men are created Muslim. They have a word for it: *fitra* (birth, or instinct). A well respected *hadith* relates that Muhammad said, "No babe is born but upon *fitra* (as a Muslim). It is his parents who make him a Jew or a Christian or a Polytheist."[4]

Western civilization has its roots in religious pluralism. At times (for example, during the Middle Ages in Western

---

[3] Qur'an 2:62.

[4] Sahih Al-Muslim, Book 033, Number 6426.

Europe) the Church did not tolerate religious diversity, but the Greek and Roman classical world which gave birth to the West was full of diverse religions and cults. The apostles were sent into this supermarket of faiths to persuade the nations that Christ was the true Logos, the exact representation of the living God and the savior of the world. They called people to follow Jesus voluntarily. It is true that periodically through the centuries the Church has committed abuses and Christian governments have forced conversions, but the New Testament is clear that the Gospel is a costly gift that is freely given, to be received through faith. The New Testament Church is a counter-culture movement which people are free to join or reject. The Judeo-Christian concept of faith is rooted in personal choice. [5]

By contrast, Muslims see religion as a system, a regime, and a society into which they are born. It is common knowledge that "Islam" means "submission to Allah" (although in the West there is a common misconception that Islam means "peace"). However, this is a superficial and only partially true definition of the word. We cannot find the complete meaning in the English-Arabic dictionary. To understand how Muslims actually define Islam we must look at the feelings, perceptions, and attitudes they associate with the term. We also need to understand the theological concepts that support this meaning.

The word "Islam" does literally denote submission, surrender, or resignation. The word "Muslim" means "one who surrenders or resigns himself." But to whom does the Muslim surrender? On the surface, it might appear that a Muslim surrenders to Allah's will, and most Christian studies of Islam make this assumption. But that is a projection based in our Christian premises about faith: what it means to be a Christian is to be a follower of Jesus, who submits to God through

---

[5] "Choose for yourselves this day whom you will serve." Joshua 24:15.

Christ. We cannot bring our Christian assumptions to our engagement with Islam without misunderstanding it.

According to the Muslim mindset, Islam is a surrender to the entire Islamic *system*. This includes obedience to Islamic law, traditions, social norms, and family wishes–as well as to religious beliefs and practices. In practice this means that every Muslim living under Islamic rule must resign himself, absolutely and unquestionably, to the customs and authority figures of his community. Islamic law is strict and does not allow for much personal choice: the Muslim must pray five times a day, he must fast during the thirty-day Ramadan fast, a woman must cover her face. Islamic law demands obedience in all aspects of life and does not tolerate personal preferences. Actually, when one submits to the "will of Allah," he is giving in to the religious leadership's interpretations of what this means. Surrender in Islam is ultimately to the dictates of Sharia law's religio-political system. It would be as if "Christian" were defined not as a follower of Christ, but as a member of the Church, or Christian society. Of course some Christians have and do understand it that way: we have our share of "cultural Christians." But there is a crucial difference between cultural Christians and Muslims. Even a cursory examination of the New Testament makes it obvious that cultural Christianity is a contradiction of the teachings of Jesus and the apostles, as well as the creeds, confessions, Church fathers, and mainstream denominations. The entire premise of those documents is that Christianity is a voluntary submission of the heart to the transforming work of Christ, and that from that submission, behavior follows, as the fruit of faith. But the social definition of religion as obedience to a culture and system is the point of Islam, and the foundation of the Muslim mindset.

Muslims argue that this marriage between civil and religious life is dictated by God. The Qur'an and the *Hadith*, they claim, contain rules pertaining to every aspect of life. From these sources religious leaders derive the laws that must govern Islamic nations. But Muslims are not uniform in their understanding of these rules. Most Sharia laws are so vague that they require extensive interpretation. Therefore, each Muslim country appoints a man called the *mufti* [6] to study and interpret the law for its own people. These rules are so changeable that the *mufti* and his team of scholars must work constantly to keep up with contemporary issues in order to find applicable references from the Qur'an or the *hadith*.

Khurshid Ahmad, a Muslim scholar from Pakistan, expresses this concept. "Departmentalization of life into different water-tight compartments, religious and secular, sacred and profane, spiritual and material, is ruled out...As Allah is One and indivisible, so is life...each aspect of life is inseparable from the other. Religious and secular are not two autonomous categories; they represent two sides of the same coin...Every human activity is given a transcendent dimension; it becomes sacred...Islam is not a religion in the Western understanding of the word...It is a faith and a way of life, a religion and a social order, a doctrine and a code of conduct, a set of values and principles and a social movement." [7]

Christians are taught that there are two worlds, spiritual and carnal. When we are born again by the Holy Spirit we be-

---

[6] The *mufti* is the one who pronounces verdicts known in Arabic as *fatawa* (singular: *fatwa*), which are legal opinions. Depending on the rank of the *mufti* and the issue at hand, a *fatwa* can be binding on Muslims or just a strong suggestion.

[7] Quoted in: Mawdudi, Abul A'la. *Towards Understanding Islam.* (International Islamic Federation of Student Organizations, 1986), page 11.

come a new creation [8] and acquire a "new man" [9] which enables us to live godly lives. From then on we are in the world but not of the world. [10] Worldly life is contrasted with spiritual life. By walking with God we are able to resist the enemy and live godly, unworldly lives. We put off the old and put on the new. This concept is directly related to our belief in original sin. We are born sinful and we need a savior.

Muslims have no such conflict between the worldly and the spiritual. Jesus' "kingdom is not of this world," [11] but Muhammad's certainly is. Personal choice is necessary to enter Christ's kingdom, but not the Umma [12] of Islam. You are a Muslim because you were born in a Muslim family. As long as you do not convert to another religion, you remain a Muslim.

I remember one day during my childhood when loud screams rang throughout the entire neighborhood. My mother jumped out of bed and rushed to the next door apartment, telling me and my siblings to stay in bed and go back to sleep. We guessed that our Muslim neighbor had just gone into labor. When the screams subsided we rushed to see the newborn baby. The house was crowded with men, women, and children offering good wishes. After the midwife washed the baby she brought him to his mother. The father came real close and whispered a few words in one ear then the other.

"What did you say to the baby?" I asked.

---

[8] "Therefore, if anyone is in Christ, he is a new creation; the old has gone, the new has come!" (2 Corinthians 5:17).

[9] "Put on the new self, created to be like God in true righteousness and holiness." (Ephesians 4:24).

[10] "They [my disciples] are still in the world...They are not of the world, even as I am not of it." (John 17:11,16).

[11] John 18:36.

[12] The Arabic word Umma refers to the global nation, community, or kingdom of Islam.

"I have just engraved into my son's permanent memory that there is no god but Allah and that Muhammad was his prophet," the proud father replied. "I want the first words my son hears to be Allah and Muhammad."

I later learned that the *Shahada* is the first pillar of Islam. From the cradle to the grave these words are repeated time and time again numerous times a day: *La Ilaha Illa Allah, Muhammad Rasul Allah* ("There is no god but Allah and Muhammad is the messenger of Allah").

The Muslim's religious worldview is not based on chosen religious beliefs and practices, as a Christian's should be. His identity as a Muslim is derived from his belonging to a Muslim family, society, culture, and political system—and conforming himself to them. As a Muslim he is convinced that he has no choice but to resign himself unquestioningly to Islamic law as it is expressed in the religio-political system under which he lives.

Iman (Belief)

When Christians think of religion they usually refer to faith in a belief system. Thus, Islam is often referred to as the Muslim faith. But there is a huge difference between the Muslim concept of faith and the Christian one.

In Christian theology, faith is defined as, "Being sure of what we hope for and certain of what we do not see." [13] Christian faith is a deliberate act of trust in God and his Word. One of my favorite hymns begins, "Standing on the promises of Christ my king." [14] We trust in the power of Christ to save us and give us a heavenly inheritance. That is not the same as the

---

[13] Hebrews 11:1.

[14] *Standing on the Promises*, Words & Music: R. Kelso Carter, in *Promises of Perfect Love*, by John Sweney and Kelso Carter (Philadelphia, PA: John J. Hood, 1886).

Muslim concept of *iman,* or belief. Three experiences in my life have helped me to understand this distinction between Christian faith and Islamic *iman.*

The first was back in the mid-1970s. I was hired to be the director of Bible translation in the Middle East and North Africa for Middle East Publications. My first task was to research the meaning of one hundred common terms between Muslims and Christians. Although my projects included Turkish, Farsi, Kurdish, and Kabyle as well as Arabic, the linguistic research was in Arabic, which is the language of the Qur'an. Several linguists and theologians were involved in helping me with this scholarly and systematic work. Additionally I consulted Muslim and Christian literature to compare and contrast how Muslims use these terms. After traveling throughout the Middle East and North Africa, I generated a lengthy report of my findings.

The second experience was from the mid-1980s. When Denver Seminary asked me to teach a course on Islam, I decided to use only Islamic sources. The textbook and required readings were all authored by Muslims from various sects. My goal was to let my students discover how Muslims define their own terms and compare them with how Christians use these terms. Often a teacher learns as much as the students as they work through the subject, and that course forced me to grapple with the material in a new way in order to explain it to my students.

The third experience was in the late 1980s when I enrolled in a post-graduate course in psycholinguistics at the University of Colorado. My paper was entitled: *Meaning Discrepancy in Common Terminology Between Muslims and Christians.* I had to delve even deeper into the subject in order to articulate it in a secular academic environment.

All of my formal research, and over forty years of ministry with Muslims, has led me to conclusions that are simple, yet difficult to explain. This is because the depth and nuance in meaning is so connected to cultural subtleties, and so much of it is "lost in translation" once it leaves Arabic. Since childhood I knew that Muslims and Christians used the same words differently, but over time I have come to appreciate just how big that gap is, and how much of our religious vocabulary it affects. The word *iman* (belief) is one of the most significant words in this respect. The Arabic Bible and the Qur'an use the same word but in vastly different ways. Book after book by Muslim scholars explaining Islam support this conclusion. For Muslims, thinking about religion is no more than acknowledgement of certain facts. When my taxi driver Adel assured me that he believes in Jesus, he did not mean that he has put his trust in Christ and the atoning work of the cross. Adel's belief in Jesus was simply accepting the fact that he was a prophet. Adel's belief in Allah was simply acknowledgment of his existence.

It is worth pointing out that in the English language the words "belief" and "disbelief" are related: one is the opposite of the other. For us, disbelief is the negation of belief. This is not so in the Arabic language. Belief and disbelief in Arabic are two unrelated words, *iman* and *kufr*. For example, I found it fascinating that Abul A'la Mawdudi (an influential Sunni Pakistani scholar), in explaining the Islamic belief system, did not start with belief. Rather he wrote first about *kufr*, which means denial or concealment. He defined a Muslim not by belief in Allah, but by saying that a Muslim is one who does not deny Allah. He went on to add that to not deny Allah is to believe in him. [15]

This emphasis on disbelief rather than belief gives us insight into the Muslim premise that all human beings are innately Muslim. Some, who are fortunate enough to be born in Muslim families, do not have to do anything except practice their religion (the Five Pillars). Those who are not born Mus-

---

[15] Mawdudi, Abul A'la, *Towards Understanding Islam*, (International Islamic Federation of Student Organizations, 1986), 21-26.

lims are still Muslims who are in "denial" or ignorance of their Islamic identity until they accept Islam. Strictly speaking, any non-Muslim who is given an opportunity to accept Islam and refuses to do so is considered a *kafir* (infidel, pronounced like "cat fur" without the "t"). This doctrine is used by some Muslim scholars to justify the qur'anic dictum to kill Christians and Jews. It is important to point out that not all Muslims believe this doctrine, or even know about it. Yet, this principle of innate Islam is a powerful presence in the minds of Muslims. Even for those who are not actively religious, there is a certain subdued state of non-denial in which they remain. This includes a fear of committing *kufr* (denial of Islam), which many Muslims must overcome before they can put their trust in Christ.

Layla had a lot of questions. I met her during a trip to North Africa last year, and I spent about four hours explaining the Gospel to her one afternoon. As I addressed each of her concerns, I kept asking, "Do you have any more questions?" It was clear that she understood the message of Christ, but something was holding her back. After all the discussion, answers, and flipping all over the Bible, she finally said, "I have no more questions, but I'm afraid of one thing. My mom told me that if I leave Islam I will go to hell. Will I go to hell?"

I looked at Youssef, a local believer who was with us. "What do you think, Youssef? Will she go to hell?" He smiled, and said "No, she'll go to heaven!"

The relief on her face was so sweet. After all the intellectual dialogue with this bright, educated woman, the last obstacle was that simple fear that had been instilled since her childhood. It had held her spiritually captive until that moment.

"Ok, I'm ready now."

Chapter 9
When You Meet a Muslim

Ideally, Christians should be witnessing to Muslims in natural settings. You may have Muslim neighbors, colleagues, co-workers, classmates, students, or teachers. Or you may meet them in shopping malls, or on buses or airplanes. It is incumbent on every Christian to reach out to them.

But what if your lifestyle or circumstances do not present you with natural opportunities to meet Muslims? Does that absolve you from obeying the Great Commission? By no means.

Seek out Opportunities

Jesus came down to us. And when he lived on earth, he did not wait for people to come to him; he went to them, in their natural settings. When he wanted Peter and Andrew to follow him, he went to them first. Jesus met his best men in their work environment: Levi at his tax collection desk, and Peter, Andrew, James, and John on the beach of Galilee.

We need selective perception. We need to actively and intentionally seek out Muslims. Do not expect Muslims to come looking for you. The mandate to reach them has been given to you by your master. Whatever it takes, we must obey the Great Commission. Just do it.

Pray for Opportunities

To help you in your search, ask God to bring you a Muslim. Ask someone to join you in prayer, or form a regular prayer group in your church or home. One of my interns was getting frustrated that he was not making progress in his witness to Muslims. I invited him to come along with me to the campus so I could show him how to seek out Muslims and start conversations with them. On our seven-minute walk to the university's student center, we prayed together. We simply asked God to lead us to Muslims who were open to the Gospel message. We also prayed that God would lead them to us. After buying our lunch and going to the cafeteria to find Muslims to share a table with, we found a man who looked like he could be a Muslim. We asked if we could sit with him and he was very welcoming.

It turned out that he was an Indonesian Muslim who was searching for a Christian to explain some things to him. An hour into a meaningful conversation that centered around Christ, he had to leave for a class. Within minutes we found another man, from Sudan. We discovered that someone else had witnessed to him the week before, and we were able to connect with him concerning issues that he was facing. It is possible, but rare, that a Muslim would come to you. You must go and seek them out.

When you pray, you become a partner with God in his work.

Seize Opportunities

When an opportunity comes, embrace it and welcome it. When you meet a Muslim, reach out to him with the love of Jesus. Sometimes the ice breaker is just a smile acknowledging the other person. Many times we meet someone in need and do nothing about it. If we do this often enough, we develop a calloused heart. Loving Jesus means reaching out to his lost sheep and bringing them into his fold. We need to take this task seriously.

One evening, I was having dinner with a mission-minded couple. They began to ask me about Islam and Muslims with great interest. That gave me the opportunity to explain some of the principles I use with Muslims when I meet them. They admitted to me that they knew a man from a Muslim country that they had not witnessed to. The woman turned to her husband and said, "This man lost his wife a few years ago. Why don't we invite him to lunch or dinner?"

Her husband loved the idea, wondering, "Why didn't we think of this before?" All it takes is awareness and willingness to look for opportunities.

The Battle is in the Heart

One evening, I had an appointment set with an imam. During our staff prayer time that day I asked the group to pray for my meeting. Todd Gunning, a staff member at Horizons, told me, "Remember that the battle is not in the mind, but in the heart." Then he prayed for me.

The imam showed up with a suitcase full of books written by liberal Christians to prove that even Christians do not believe in the infallibility of the Bible. The books were piled up in front of him to intimidate me. This was not going to be easy. In my experience, it is futile to argue with someone who has made up his mind. How could I overcome all the biblical criticism that he had heard from Christian liberals and Muslim polemics? I imagined that this was going to take hours of heated argument. I would have had to discredit the liberal Christian theologians and prove the authenticity of the Bible based on a variety of internal and external evidence. Josh McDowell has written a number of very helpful scholarly books on this subject, and I wondered whether I should have brought some of those to the meeting.

I prayed again and said, "Lord, I need you." As I prayed, Todd's words popped into my head: "The battle is in the heart, not the mind." Instead of the apologetic arguments I could have shared with the imam, I decided to do something I have often done in similar situations: I asked a question.

"Do you pray five times a day?" I asked the imam.

"Yes, of course I do," he replied.

"What else do you do so you will go to heaven?"

"I try to practice the Five Pillars." He began to explain, "Prayer, fasting..."

I gently interrupted. "Are there other things, or only five practices?"

He did not miss a beat. "As a Muslim I am required to follow God's laws (Sharia)."

"How many laws are there?" I asked him. "And how many of them do you obey well?"

"There are many many laws...see, the Qur'an and the *Hadith*..."

He began to explain that Islamic Sharia is based on the authority of the Qur'an and the *Hadith*. It contains rules for everything in life, even instructions on how to brush your teeth and go to the toilet.

"How many of these laws are you able to obey?" I asked. "Would you say fifty percent? Ninety percent?"

He seemed a bit bewildered by my question. His eyes began to roam around the room as if he was trying to come up with a good answer.

"I have done all the Five Pillars and I try to obey as many rules as I can. No one can do all of them..."

I interrupted again. "Why would God require of you more than you can do? Isn't that cruel?"

We discussed this for a while. I pointed out how many laws of Moses there were, and that the Jewish religious leaders added even more laws of their own, making the religion even harder to follow. The Bible teaches us that the problem with man is not that he does not obey God, but that he is not *capable* of obeying God; he will always come up short. The imam's contribution to the discussion was consistent with his belief that, "We do our best and God does the rest."

I changed my tone, and asked an even more personal question. "So, how do you know that you will be going to heaven?"

The imam replied honestly. "This is not up to me to decide. I do my best, but Allah has the final word." He admitted that there is no way human beings will ever know their destiny, and that all we can do is hope for Allah's mercy. This was a moment of discovery for the imam. All the books on the table, with all their arguments, had faded away. He was no longer trying to prove anything. We had come face to face with the most important question of his life: his eternal destiny. Realizing that I had just touched a chord deep within him, I thanked God for this milestone and asked the Lord to open his heart. When you are witnessing to someone, there comes a moment when you need to make the issue very personal. This was that moment.

"Would you like to know what the Bible says about how to receive forgiveness from sin and what qualifies you to enter God's presence in heaven?"

This was the most earnest and intimate moment in our conversation. The imam reflected for a few seconds before calmly and sincerely responding that indeed he would like to know. This gave me an open door straight into his heart. I opened the Bible and began to share with him the great news of the free gift of forgiveness and grace from God that we can be assured of through Jesus. I told him that none of us are worthy of heaven because heaven is a holy place and we are sinners. Only by grace can we be saved. [1] God did the work of salvation because we cannot. He paid a price which was too steep for us to pay. The imam's heart absorbed the good news like a sponge absorbs water.

This encounter was typical of the conversations I have had with many Muslims–with widely different results. Some are convicted. Others are cold and reject anything I say. Others are interested but seem to be unaffected. One lesson we can

---

[1] Ephesians 2:7-10.

draw from this experience is that some people are more open to the Holy Spirit than others.

Offer Hospitality and Friendship

Christians are commanded to be hospitable to strangers and people from other countries by treating them as we would our own people. The Israelites were told that, "The stranger who resides with you shall be to you as the native among you, and you shall love him as yourself." [2]

God reminded the early Christians not to "neglect to show hospitality to strangers." [3] Hospitality has played a role in the conversion story of almost every former Muslim. In our ministry, we have matched hundreds of international students with Christian friendship partners over the years. As a result, we have seen a percentage of them respond positively and end up receiving Christ. One such story is of a Saudi woman who was befriended by her college classmates. Eventually, she received a Bible and began to attend church. As she read his word and interacted with many believers, God began to work in her heart. Within a couple of years she was ready to take a huge step away from Islam to Christ.

Hospitality is one of the most enjoyable ministries I have done. The beauty of it is that you can do it as a family. My wife and I invited a young Kuwaiti student for dinner one evening. He had such rapport with our children that when the time came for me to drive him back to the campus, they wanted to come along. My daughter, Noelle, who was four at the time, tried to stop him from leaving by singing:

> *Stop! And let me tell you what the Lord has done for me.*
> *He forgave my sins and he saved my soul,*

---

[2] Leviticus 19:34. See also 1 Timothy 3:2, Titus 1:8, Romans 12:13, and 3 John 1:8.

[3] Hebrews 13:2.

He cleansed my heart and he made me whole.
Stop! And let me tell you what the Lord has done for me.

It was an incredible opportunity to explain this song that came from the lips of a child.

But hospitality should not be limited to international students. There is a chance you will meet a Muslim in your neighborhood, recreation center, school, work, or in the park. Remember that true love is taking a step toward someone. Sadly, sixty to eighty percent of international students living in the USA never get invited into an American home, let alone a Christian home. Many Muslims living in the USA are seeking friendship from anyone who will offer it. If we will simply be a friend to them, we may be able to introduce them to our friend, Jesus.

Use the Bible

The Word of God is powerful. We should always keep a Bible handy, and at least one that we could give away when the opportunity arises. Having a searchable Bible text on a smartphone or iPod can be very useful as well. When we get into a discussion with a Muslim friend, we can pull out the Bible and read a relevant passage on that topic. We should share the spiritual lessons God is teaching us, freely and often, opening the Bible to read the passage from which we learned each lesson. This will not only open the Word of God to a Muslim in a non-threatening way, but it will also show him what it means to have a relationship with the living God. The more consistent you are in reading the Bible, the more verses will pop into your mind during conversation.

If I have a Bible in my hand when talking to a Muslim, I almost always open it to show them the verses I am mentioning. Even if it takes two minutes to find the verse, it's worth it; it really does make a tremendous difference. A lot of people quote scripture from their memory without looking at the

Bible. Memorization is good for you and your own contemplation of God's Word. It can certainly impress the person you are witnessing to, and that's not always bad. It can show that you are learned and take the Bible seriously. But that's not the point of evangelism; the point is to let the word of God speak to them. Often I have opened the Bible with a Muslim only to have them grab it and leave me alone–they wanted to read more. There is a curiosity in the heart of every Muslim about the Bible. They want to know what the Bible says because they've been told, "Oh, the Bible is no good. It's bad." But in most cases they've never actually seen one.

I have had missionaries tell me, "I don't know, he's a Muslim–should I give him a Bible?" Yes! What else are you going to give him? A Qur'an? A Buddha? Give him a Bible![4] Let him read in the Bible as you help him navigate through verses and passages about the love of God, eternal life, the assurance of salvation, and God's promises–the things that they don't have. Parables of Jesus can be the most captivating.

Tell the Story of the Gospel

The message of the good news of God's love is very simple. The more complicated we make it, the less likely it is that a Muslim will respond. The simpler the message, the more powerful. Many Christian workers witness by sharing abstract facts and truths. "God is a just God. His justice and love are satisfied in Christ on the cross." Even though this is true, it often does not communicate anything intimate to the heart of the person you are sharing with. Share the same truth in the context of your own testimony, or a testimony of someone you know or have read about. Muslims need to know that God

---

[4] In many cases the most effective thing to give is just one of the gospels, or a booklet with topical scripture portions. It can be overwhelming for a Muslim to receive the entire Bible without knowing where to start.

loves them, that they can have a personal relationship with him, that their sins can be forgiven, and that they can have eternal life through Jesus. They can become children of God, joining his international family of believers.

If you have reached the point in the conversation where it is appropriate, you might pick an appropriate parable and ask a Muslim, "Have you heard of this story that Jesus told?" Or you might ask, "How do you know whether you are going to heaven?" Let them reflect on the question, "What shall I do to go to heaven?" In following up on that question I have often used the example of an insurance policy: if we can count on our insurance agency, shouldn't we be able to count on God to be faithful to his promises?

Deal with One Person at a Time. Avoid the Peer Pressure of Groups

A Saudi student came to my office one day asking for a Bible. Before I gave him one, I asked him to tell me his story, and he revealed a little-known fact. He said that many Shiite Muslims in Saudi Arabia are discovering their Christian roots. He went on to tell me that the southern region of Najran, close to Yemen, used to be all Christian. After a few hours of discussion he went away with a large Arabic-English Bible. He later called me and told me that he spoke to his friends and cousins about me, and they wanted me to come and explain Christianity to them. Firas, a Horizons staff member from Iraq, and I went to meet with them. They spread out a banquet table of venison cooked by Saudi women, who hid in the other room. Then we sat on the floor cushions and they began to ask us questions. We did our best to answer their questions. Most of them were very interested. One however, took it upon himself to protect the others from our "deception." He spoiled the atmosphere with his arguments. It turned out that he was an Islamist. This one bad apple spoiled the bunch, and none of the others were going to stick their necks out by showing genuine interest.

The Saudi man who came to me for a Bible did not call again and never returned my calls. This is just one of many experiences that taught me to be careful about witnessing to a Muslim in the presence of his or her peers. Groups can be useful for determining which individuals are open, but sometimes when it comes to more serious sharing, you need to find a time and place to be alone with your friend.

Do Not Invite Muslims to Church until They Are Ready– Home Groups Are Often Better.

One of the saddest stories I have ever heard took place during the late 1940's in Greeley, Colorado. An Egyptian student named Sayyed was attending the University of Northern Colorado. He was invited to a church lock-in, without knowing what to expect. He was offended by loose gender relationships which he perceived as immoral. Upon his return to Egypt he wrote an article entitled, "The America I have Seen," in which he related his experience at the church and many other negative experiences and observations. He went on to become the leading intellectual for the Muslim Brotherhood who shaped the ideology of Osama Bin Ladin's Al Qaeda and other terrorist organizations. He is considered the father of Islamic extremism because of his great influence through his books and teachings. He was killed in 1966, executed by the Egyptian government.

An invitation to church doesn't have to be disastrous. After spending many hours a week with Hussein from Pakistan, he begged me to take him to church. He loved it so much that he continued to come for several months until he returned to his home country. He developed so many relationships in the church that he once proudly told me, "I have more invitations for dinners than there are days for the rest of my stay in the US." He went home with great feelings about the love and affection he has experienced. We can only wish that Sayyed Qutb would have been shown so much acceptance and love.

Do Not Argue

I loved to argue when I was younger. I was armed with Bible verses which I fired at my opponents like bullets–whether I was talking to Muslims, Jehovah's witnesses, or nominal Christians. Wherever I could find someone to argue with, I was ready to beat them with my well-prepared arguments. But I only made them angry by showing them that their leaders had deceived them, twisted the scriptures, and quoted verses out of context. I didn't understand why they wouldn't want to know that I had decoded the secret of their deception. It took years before I realized how fruitless this method was. I eventually realized that people responded better when I engaged them instead of debating them, and I was able to lead more of them to Christ.

If you get into an argument, just stop. Calm down. Be quiet. Stay focused. Relax. Pray. God is in charge. It is OK for the person who is arguing with you to talk without you interrupting. Consider it your opportunity to learn how he or she feels and thinks. This gives you some clues as to how you may be able to respond. Do not interrupt. Be patient. Your friend will appreciate you for listening, but also he may soon "run out of gas" if you don't keep trying to interject–although some people can talk all day without stopping.

When it seems that argument is inevitable, I often begin to tell a story, a parable, or my testimony. Usually people can argue with your ideas and opinions but they cannot argue with a story or experience. When the blind man in John 9 was questioned about the credibility of Jesus, he simply stated, "I was blind and now I see." A person may disregard your personal experience, but he cannot disprove it. Let them say what they want. Do not interrupt.

After the person dumps on you, ask them if they are ready to let you speak. Rather than arguing back at them, give your testimony. Tell about any answered prayers. Changed lives and answered prayers are evidence of the living God. This should defuse the argument. Tell stories and parables instead of dumping information.

Pray

Anyone involved in ministry to Muslims knows that there is a spiritual battle raging. We need to pray that God will open the eyes of Muslims to see his revelation. Our prayer should be that God would lead us to Muslims who are hungry for the Gospel. Further, consider joining or starting a prayer group that focuses on Islam and the Muslim world. I have found also that praying with a Muslim impacts them greatly. By the way, if you have Muslims over for a meal, do not just say a quick prayer. This is a great opportunity to demonstrate how Christians talk to God.

Share Current Answers to Prayer

Muslims need to see how God is working in our lives. When they see God working out a situation beyond our control or see us responding in faith to something Jesus says, they may become aware that they need him too. One Afghan Muslim was not open to the Gospel until his eight-year old daughter got seriously ill. A Christian pastor stopped at his flower shop and offered to pray for the girl. The man agreed without understanding what this pastor really meant. The pastor received a phone call the following day from the father, who said he wanted to know more about Jesus–the one who instantly healed his daughter. This wonderful Afghan brother in the Lord told this story when he came to one of our conferences for former Muslims. When you hear of a story like this one, share it with your Muslim friends.

Give More Literature, Videos, and Bibles

The more literature and scriptures are given out, the more Muslims come to Christ. When I began my project to translate the Bible into Sorani Kurdish in 1973, the Kurds were unable to read the Bible in their language. It had not been translated. Shortly after the release of just one gospel (Luke), many Kurds began to know Christ and believed in him. Following the printing of the full New Testament, thousands of Kurds responded positively. A Christian worker needs to have gospels and New Testaments available all the time. Leave a box of scripture portions and Bibles in the trunk of the car, in your computer bag, back pack, or purse.

Work as a Team

Most of the time, it takes many Christians to lead one Muslim to Christ. Muslims who have had more interaction with Christians tend to respond better. I know Christian workers–both in the US and on the mission field–who do not introduce their friend to other Christians for fear of losing them. This "sheep stealing" mentality is incredibly damaging. Introduce your friend to other Christians. Invite him or her to your home in addition to cafés and restaurants. Take them on a hike, or go shopping with them. Without a relationship our Gospel is words. It is your love in action that will make the difference.

Be Persistent

Evangelism to Muslims can be frustrating. Many workers have given up and have begun to work with more responsive people, such as the Chinese. Should we write off a fifth of the world's population–who do not know the salvation of God through Jesus Christ–just because they are difficult to reach?

Jesus warned us that there would be perils along the way, that we might be persecuted and even rejected. Jesus also warned that of the many people we tell about him, only a few will respond. [5] Instead of looking for the easy way out, we must be resilient in our approach to Muslims. If we give up too soon, we may waste all the preparatory time we have invested in these relationships. "Let us not become weary in doing good, for at the proper time we will reap a harvest if we do not give up." [6]

Too often we expect Muslims to respond immediately, so we do not allow the Holy Spirit time to work in their hearts. As we interact with Muslims, they may be watching our lives and hearing our words, and they may not be showing any response. Below the surface, however, they may be asking deep and difficult questions. We must pray that the Holy Spirit will convict them and draw them to himself. We plow, plant, and water, but God causes the growth. [7]

As we are faithful in our witness and are patient in waiting for God's time, we will reap in due time. Do not lose heart.

---

[5] "For many are invited, but few are chosen." Matthew 22:14.

[6] Galatians 6:9.

[7] 1 Corinthians 3:6, Mark 4:26-29.

Chapter 10
The Art of Asking Questions

The day my mother died was one of the most tragic days of my life. As the youngest of her four children, she and I were close, and I was devastated. For days, I mourned and cried as though my world had fallen apart. Trying to make sense of what happened, we discovered that her death at the age of fifty-two was completely unnecessary. It boiled down to a wrong diagnosis. The doctor had failed to ask her certain questions about what medications she was taking at the time and prescribed a blood thinner, which was just the opposite of what she needed. A few questions asked by the doctor could have saved my mother's life.

As Christians, we are in the business of saving lives from the claws of spiritual death. Therefore, it is extremely important that we develop the skill–and art–of diagnosis so that our message will bring healing to the broken-hearted, freedom to the captives, and life to the spiritually dead.

A medical doctor does not prescribe the same remedy for every patient. First, he asks diagnostic questions to understand the medical condition of his patient, and if necessary he does a physical examination or more extensive testing. In this section we are going to look into the art of asking good questions, which will help us understand our Muslim friends and enable us to share the message that speaks to their needs. We will also touch on how to answer questions asked by Muslims.

Engaging Muslims requires that we understand them. No Muslim is exactly like any other. Each has a different background, various needs, and special problems. You cannot expect one approach to work well with every individual. We must ask questions, just as a medical doctor does, to discover what they know, how they feel, and what they need. Most importantly, it is critical to assess their level of interest and openness. Too many evangelists do not truly engage the people they are evangelizing. They know in advance that all Muslims need to hear about Jesus, so they just talk and talk without pausing to gather any feedback along the way. This is dumping information, not communicating. When you ask people questions you demonstrate that you care about them, while also gathering the information you need in order to speak into their lives with appropriate wisdom.

There is no 'cookie cutter,' one-size-fits-all method; you just have to explore and find out what works best for the person you are working with.

Ask Personal Questions

Take genuine interest in your Muslim friends, and show it through asking personal questions about their life, family, work, and studies. Get to know them in the same way that you get to know anyone else: by showing interest in their lives. This is an important part of building trust. Identify areas of struggle. Be personal. Ask about their lives. Consider questions like these, that lead to wide-ranging, personal conversations:

- *How many brothers and sisters do you have?*

- *What are some things you like to do in your spare time?*

- *Tell me about your family.*

- *What are some goals you'd like to accomplish in your life?*

Also, try to look for (and make) the right opportunities to ask more pointed questions:

- *Do you have any questions about Jesus or the Bible?*

- *Have you ever had a dream of Jesus?*

- *Have you ever read the Injeel (Gospel)?*
- *But be careful not to ask too much too soon. Don't make it feel like an interrogation. Be natural. It is extremely important to ask your Muslim friends questions that will give them an opportunity to share their heart with you. Before you can do that, they need to feel that they can trust you. This takes time.*

Listen Genuinely before You Speak

Asking questions is not like filling out a questionnaire. Rather, the purpose of your questions is to learn about the person sitting across from you. This requires that you listen genuinely to personal needs and address them with a prayerful attitude.

Hani was an Egyptian Muslim who had a fairly good knowledge of Islam. He was required to memorize large portions of the Qur'an in his childhood and youth. When he met another Arab who was a Christian, Hani set out to convert him to Islam. He had such confidence in his religion that he thought a few arguments would persuade his fellow Arab of the glories of Islam. The two met several times, sometimes discussing–often arguing over–topics such as the reliability of the scriptures, the Trinity, the sonship of Jesus, the crucifixion, and so on.

To his shock, Hani discovered that Issam was a strong believer in Christ and that he had reasonable answers. But the bigger shock came when Hani began to see that Issam was more honest than he was. When Issam did not know the answer, he promised that he would study the topic and come back with one. On the other hand, Hani found himself fabricating answers. This honesty in his Christian friend and awareness of his own dishonesty challenged him to consider the claims of Christianity.

Do Not Ask about Islam

Ahmed was invited to dinner by his friendship family. He was new in the US, and was excited to be in the home of a Christian. He had never even met a Christian before starting his exchange program, so he was curious to see what they are like and learn what they believe. Tom, the host, began to bombard Ahmed with questions about Islam. Ahmed was embarrassed that he did not know Islam well enough to answer most of the questions. When he returned home, he realized that he had been a weak Muslim and decided to begin learning about his religion. He went to the mosque for answers. Once there, he began to read the Qur'an and perform the prayer rituals, which he hadn't done more than a few times since he was young. In the process, he asked the imam about the questions that Tom had asked him. He called Tom and asked to meet with him to share the answers with him. He now was prepared to "evangelize" his Christian friend. Ahmed lost interest in learning about Christianity and began to share about Islam with Tom and other Christians. The window of time during which he was open had passed, and Tom was no longer able to witness to him.

When your goal is to witness to your Muslim friend, it is understandable that you may want to engage him or her by asking questions about religion and faith. However, this can be perilous as it runs the risk of causing the Muslim friend to talk about the glories of Islam. More and more Muslims are being taught to argue with Christians. The mosque offers seminars and books that attack Christianity and the Bible. They are given ammunition against Christians in order to protect them from what they perceive as conversion attempts.

Try to avoid questions that may give the Muslim a platform to convince you of the virtues of Islam. This is one of the most common mistakes Christians commit in relating to Muslims. Try to forget that the person is a Muslim: treat him or her as an ordinary person. Most Muslims who are usually not religious will put up a religious front when engaged in a discussion about Islam, whereas they may never bring it up if you don't.

Engaging through Questions

In the summer of 2008, my two older sons, André and Pierre, and I led a team to witness to Arabs in a park in Dearborn, Michigan. This was the practical element of our annual *Engaging Islam* training conference. Peter, one of the students who had never witnessed to a Muslim before, began to speak to an Iraqi man. He had a very clear and theologically accurate presentation of the Gospel. As the coach, I intervened and asked the Iraqi man, "Did you understand what Peter just told you?"

"Sure, I understood," said Fareed.

"Can you tell me what he told you?"

Fareed didn't hesitate. He repeated what he had heard, not what Peter had actually said: "He said that we need to do good works to please God."

Peter was shocked; those were neither his words nor intent. I reminded him of the lesson we had covered that day in class: we must engage Muslims, not just deliver the Gospel message to them. So I instructed Peter to open to the scripture that he had quoted and let Fareed read it in the Arabic-English New Testament we had just given him. Peter turned to John 14:6, and Fareed read, "Jesus answered, 'I am the way and the truth and the life. No one comes to the Father except through me.' " By now Peter realized that Fareed wasn't getting it. He had read the words, but somehow wasn't processing them. Peter was stuck, so I stepped in with some questions to clarify matters. "Fareed, Jesus said 'I am the way.' What does that mean?"

He thought for a moment. "Umm, like a road?"

"Yes," I nodded. "The road to where?"

Fareed looked genuinely confused. "Uhh..."

"The road to God," I said, connecting the dots for him.

"Ahh!" I could see Fareed's face brighten with understanding.

The conversation changed from a lecture to an engagement. I asked Fareed to tell us what he understood about each word in the verse and different people on the team began to help him with his questions. True communication began to take place. My son Pierre took him aside and spent two hours reading and explaining the Gospel to him as the rest of us looked for other Arabs to talk to.

There are several lessons we can learn from this encounter:

1. Even if the passage seems simple to you, don't assume others understand it.

2. Let them read the Bible to you, and let them try to explain it to you.

3. Make sure they understand what you're talking about by asking follow up questions. Don't simply ask, "Do you understand?" Many will say yes to avoid embarrassment.

4. Give them chances to try answering your questions. Let their process of discovery unfold as you give them hints and suggestive questions.

Answering Difficult Questions

Asking questions is only part of communication; you need to allow your friend opportunities to ask you questions as well. In fact, some of the most valuable times I have spent with Muslims were when I was answering their questions. But don't try to answer questions unless you know the answer. Be willing to say, "I don't know."

When you are faced with questions which you do not know how to answer, do not panic. I usually just turn to God for help, and–to my surprise–God gives it to me. Do not feel that you have to be an expert who knows it all. In a relaxed manner, you can steer the conversation to another topic. I have found that sometimes it is better to change the subject and discuss another topic of interest. Do not feel obligated to answer every question; Jesus certainly didn't feel bad for avoiding traps or answering people's questions with a question of his own. It's also not wrong to ignore the question and just say what you want to say. Conversation is an art, so you must develop your own ways of guiding discussions in order to make them as fruitful as possible. Just as in pruning a fruit tree, it's important to cut off unfruitful topics that branch too far off course.

Arta interrupted me as I was teaching in a church in Kosova. She wanted to know the meaning of the term "Son of God." Knowing that this could distract from the topic at hand I asked her, "Would you like the two-minute answer or the two-hour answer?" Fortunately, she chose the short answer and she never asked that question again. My question showed her that the topic was very deep, which meant my quick answer could not be judged for being so short. I often use one of these answers when I am asked a difficult question:

- *"There is a more important question to ask."*

- *"I want to answer you, but this is advanced. You need to know the basics first."*

- *"Before I can answer your question, can you first answer this question for me?"*

- *"How do you think I would answer that question?"*

- *"I'd like to tell you a story..."*

Creating Opportunities to Share

Taking your Muslim friends to concerts, films, drama, talks, and other events having to do with Christ can be quite effective. It helps them enjoy the journey of discovery, and the activity makes the atmosphere casual and comfortable. Even though Muslims can feel inhibited in groups, under certain circumstances a social setting can create a positive dynamic for sharing.

For example, during the Christmas season in 2008, my son Zef, my wife Joy, and I sang Handel's *Messiah* with a local church choir in Colorado. It was a glorious performance, with a hundred voices and a thirty-piece orchestra. Along with a veteran missionary who lived in the area, we invited a number of Muslims, and almost thirty of them showed up. After the performance, we were all invited to the missionary's house for a late dinner. Among the twenty-two who came were several Iranians and Turks, plus six Saudis. The idea was for Christians and Muslims to mingle together and chat for a couple of hours. We had no clue what God had planned for that night.

After everyone ate and sat down, I shared an overview of the message of *The Messiah* and gave opportunities for them to ask questions. We were amazed at how much these men and women understood. They asked questions like, *"Who is the child who was born? What does the word 'Messiah' mean? What about Hallelujah? What is 'Good tidings?"* I couldn't help notice their admiration of Zef for his brilliant baritone rendering of "The Trumpet Shall Sound." It was obvious that these students were awed by the experience, and they wanted to understand it better.

That night, I told them that Handel's *Messiah* captures the essence of God's cosmic plan of salvation. With musical genius, Handel brought the scriptures to life, highlighting the major messianic prophecies and connecting them to the life of Christ in the gospels. The message of redemption through the sacrificial work of Christ on the cross was all laid out, from the Old Testament through the Revelation of John.

I explained that all of the words sung in the piece were from the Bible, and taught them a bit about when these prophecies were recorded–that Isaiah clearly prophesied about the Messiah seven hundred years before he came! We spent time opening several of these verses, reading them aloud, and explaining their significance. I made sure that I did not talk for more than a few minutes without either asking a question or letting them ask me a question. That type of dialogue allows true communication.

At one point I shared about God's fatherly love for us and his desire to adopt us as his children–his heirs of eternal life. I pointed to my son, Zef, glanced at the six Saudi men surrounding him, and said, "When my wife and I die, this young man, my son, and his three siblings will inherit everything we own. Our house, our cash, and everything we have will be theirs."

I joked with one of the Saudis: "I like you. You are a nice man. But I assure you that you will not inherit even one dollar from me." Everyone laughed. "In the same way, my son will not share in the inheritance you will receive from your father."

As the whole group chuckled and joked, I continued, "Do you know why?" Ashraf was quick to answer, "Because he is your son, and I am not your son."

He got it.

Zef picked up where I left off and explained to them that God does not long for us to be religious. He wants a relationship with us: a father-son relationship. He wants to adopt us as sons and daughters, and let us inherit everything he has. This conversation went on for several hours as the students asked more questions, trying to understand this concept, which was completely new to them. In turn, I asked them questions to gauge their understanding and what they still needed to know.

From nine o'clock in the evening, when we sat down to talk, until two in the morning, none of the twenty-two guests left. None of them argued or brought up issues of conflict. It would have been foolish to bring down the evening from the sublime to the ridiculous. I was finally exhausted and closed the meeting, but it was amazing, a night to remember and cherish.

That *Messiah* discussion was not about doctrine and ideology. It was not about politics and conflicting world agendas. Nor was it about religion or culture. The discussions went beyond ideas to something more lofty. It was all about Jesus the Messiah, and God's perfect and love-filled plan to restore his lost children to the original image in which they were created. There was music, there was beauty, there was imagery, there was history, there was love, there was life. God was in the center. To Him be the glory.

Engaging Muslims does not have to be a chore. It can be quite enjoyable. Knowing how to ask and answer questions is an effective tool. It brings you and your Muslim friend closer and allows true engagement to occur.

Look and Pray for the Right Time to Ask Your Friend to Make a Decision to Follow Jesus

In their eagerness to get quick results, many people invite Muslims to accept Christ too early in the relationship. "Strike while the iron is hot," they may tell themselves. There was a time when I thought that way as well. I wanted to make sure my Muslim friend was saved before something bad happened. I would passionately warn, "What if–God forbid–you leave this place and a car hits you? Repent now and be safe." Usually those who accept Christ too quickly, without understanding the implications and the possible cost of their decision, do not last long in the faith. Easy come, easy go.

For many years now I have encouraged my contacts to take their time, making sure that they really understand the

Gospel and the call to accept it. I give them books to read, videos to watch, CD's to listen to, and internet sites to visit. Those are aids, but not substitutes for a relationship; literature and media cannot replace personal time with them. So I offer to read the Bible with them, and answer their questions. When a heart seems ripe, I gently ask them if they are ready.

Recently in North Africa, a young woman named Mounira told me she was ready. But I kept asking her questions. "Explain to me your understanding of the cross. Did Jesus have to die? Why did he die and not save us some other way? Can you explain sin to me? What about you? Why do you want to accept Christ? Are you aware of what might happen to you if your family found out? Do you think dying for Christ is worthwhile?"

This took a few hours to go through. When she did not know how to answer a question, I opened the Bible and gently explained. It went by quickly as I interjected some light talk and jokes. But in the end Mounira was ready. "Are you really ready?" I asked. She enthusiastically responded positively. We got on our knees and–in her own words–she repented from her sin, invited Christ to enter her life, and committed her life to him. When we rose to our feet she was bubbling with joy, jumping up and down, and hugging all four other people in the room.

A year later, Mounira is still going on with the Lord and is being discipled by local missionaries with whom we work.

Chapter 11
The Umma and the Church

We could hear him shrieking in his strong Pakistani accent from all the way across the mosque. This imam was trying to impress my Denver Seminary students. He had picked a number of men to come and help him give us a guided tour of a local Islamic center.

"See?" he exclaimed. "All these men around me? This one is from Algeria, this one is from Sudan, this one is from Indonesia, and this one is from Egypt. We belong to many countries, but we are one *Umma!*"

Does that sound like the Islamic version of the universal ("holy, catholic") Church that we affirm in the Apostle's Creed? To someone who hasn't spent years conversing with Muslims about their religion, it might seem so. But I knew that this was exactly not what the imam meant. It was an opportunity to explain to him that Jesus came not to establish an earthly kingdom, but God's rule over our hearts. Jesus affirmed to his disciples, "The kingdom of God is within you,"[1] and, "My kingdom is not of this world. If it were, my servants would fight to prevent my arrest by the Jews."[2]

But one of the imam's assistants blurted out, "I am first a Muslim, then Algerian. The Sharia of God is our law. The *Umma* does not submit to non-Muslim rulers. One day Islam will rule the world!" He took a deep breath as he looked at his colleagues. With deep emotion he continued, "At that time we will not be Algerians, Egyptians, Pakistanis or Americans. We

---

[1] Luke 17:21.

[2] John 18:36.

will all be Muslim, *inshallah*."[3] The imam echoed and the others joined him, shouting: "*Allahu akbar*"[4] ("Allah is greater").

What a contrast between the missions of Muhammad and Jesus! I badly wanted to show him that our ultimate goal is not earth but heaven. I longed to help him understand that Christians, who let God rule their hearts, belong to different earthly nations, yet find true citizenship in the invisible Kingdom of God, without physical borders or political agendas. The Church is multiethnic and multilingual, but it is primarily a gathering of people from all nations, tribes, and languages, bound by faith in God through Christ. It is a spiritual "holy nation, a royal priesthood."[5] It occurred to me that anything I would have said would have fallen on deaf ears. I figured, "What's the use of arguing?" So I gave my students a chance to ask the imam other questions.

That was before September 11, 2001.

On a different continent, and after 9-11, I was conducting our *Engaging Islam* training in Pretoria, South Africa. My students were primarily pastors from various African countries, and one day I took them to the largest mosque in the city. It was Friday, and the mosque was packed. We stood against the wall in the back to observe, and the imam did not realize that we were there. After the usual recitations and prayers in Arabic, he shifted to English, and for fifteen minutes gave the fiery khitba (sermon). The message was loud and passionate, like a military commander rallying his troops for battle. "Our *Umma* is in crisis! See what the enemies of Islam have done to our unity? They have waged wars against us in Afghanistan, in Iraq, and all over the world to humiliate us and defeat us." He

---

[3] *Inshallah* is an Arabic expression literally means "If God wills it."

[4] *Allahu akbar* is one thing the imam sings in the call to prayer five times a day. The expression is used often in demonstrations and as a war cry to affirm invoke Allah's victory.

[5] 1 Peter 2:9.

incited anger and hatred in the hearts of the hundreds of Muslims who sat nodding on the beautifully carpeted floor. They affirmed his message, their cries of, "*Allahu akbar*" reverberating throughout the spacious hall.

What came next was shocking. The imam switched back into Arabic and began to pray for the destruction of America and Europe, even using the phrase "Christian nations." "Oh Allah, destroy their homes, their families, and their countries. Oh Allah, bring on them disasters, tsunamis, hurricanes, floods, and diseases. Oh, Allah, give us victory over our enemies." I looked at my students, who looked confused even though they didn't understand his words.

He ended with a mantra-like phrase, repeated over and over, the crowd chanting with him in Arabic: "*Allahuma, unsur Ummat al-Islam.*" ("O Allah give victory to the *Umma* of Islam.")

We waited to talk to him afterward. I introduced my class and explained that we would like to ask him some questions. He called two other imams and invited us to sit on the floor in the entrance of the mosque. After welcoming us with a big smile, he invited us to ask him whatever we wished.

This was my opportunity. "I noticed that during your prayer, you spent five minutes cursing Christians..." The imam paused, smiled, and said, "I'm sorry, you must have misunderstood me." He obviously thought I was a westerner. I repeated my observation, but this time in Arabic. As I spoke, his face turned red with embarrassment. He turned around and began to whisper with his colleagues, as if they were trying to come up with a unified answer. It must have been an entire minute before he turned back to us. Somewhat sheepishly, he responded, "The Qur'an tells us that the *Umma* of Islam is to conquer the world." I responded, "Do you see these men with me? They are pastors from many African nations. Did you know that from their pulpits every Sunday they encourage their people to love Muslims and pray for them? Jesus taught us, 'Bless those who curse you, pray for those who mistreat you.'[6] All around the world, Christians pray blessings upon the Muslims of the world."

The atmosphere was electric as the other pastors began to share their hearts with the three imams. The contrast between the dreams of Jesus and Muhammad could not have been more stark. Jesus told Pilate, "My kingdom is not of this world." He died with other men's spit in his beard. Muhammad beheaded those who resisted his theocratic regime. He dreamed of an *Umma* that would bring the whole world under Islamic rule through imposing Sharia law.

The leading imam seemed shaken by the amazing love that was pouring out of the pastors' mouths. He told me that he would like to sit with me one-on-one and talk about this. We agreed on a time and place to meet the next day. My host gave him my contact information. But as he reached into his pocket to give me his card with his phone number and address, the imam next to him intervened. He snatched the business card from his hand and said, "There will not be any such meetings."

The next day I went to the place we had discussed meeting at, just in case he would show up. Sadly, he did not. I knew why.

The *Umma* is Not the Muslim Version of the Universal Church

Jesus knew the aspirations of a religious nation. The Jews of his day had been awaiting a messiah who would be a general, a lawgiver, and a king. They wanted to triumph over the Romans and gain their independence. When this simple, self-appointed rabbi from Nazareth began teaching and performing miracles, he attracted huge crowds. Many of his followers hoped that he would organize them into an insurrection against the Roman occupiers. They longed for him to reestab-

---

[6] Luke 6:28.

lish the earthly throne of David and to make Israel rich and powerful again, as it had been under Solomon. Even his most intimate followers expected him to demonstrate his messiahship through Jewish theocratic nationalism, and thus to bring the Kingdom of Heaven onto earth through their special nation. Two of his closest apostles, James and John, misunderstood what kind of kingdom Jesus came to build. Their confusion and Jesus' response to it highlights the difference between the Church of Jesus and the *Umma* of Muhammad:

> *Then James and John, the sons of Zebedee, came to him. "Teacher," they said, "we want you to do for us whatever we ask."*
>
> *"What do you want me to do for you?" he asked.*
>
> *They replied, "Let one of us sit at your right and the other at your left in your glory.*
>
> *"You don't know what you are asking," Jesus said. "Can you drink the cup I drink or be baptized with the baptism I am baptized with?"*
>
> *"We can," they answered. Jesus said to them, "You will drink the cup I drink and be baptized with the baptism I am baptized with, but to sit at my right or left is not for me to grant. These places belong to those for whom they have been prepared."*
>
> *When the ten heard about this, they became indignant with James and John. Jesus called them together and said, "You know that those who are regarded as rulers of the Gentiles lord it over them, and their high officials exercise authority over them. Not so with you. Instead, whoever wants to become great among you must be your servant, and whoever wants to be first must be slave of all. For even the Son of Man*

did not come to be served, but to serve, and to give his life as a ransom for many." [7]

Unlike Jesus, Muhammad deliberately raised expectations of religious nationalism in his followers. The Qur'an praises the Muslims: "You are the best of the nations raised up for (the benefit of) men." [8] Muhammad did not puncture these expectations. Rather, he fed them by leading armies, fighting battles, and claiming booty from the defeated. He called himself a prophet, but he functioned as a ruler. He destroyed enemies, enlarged the secular power of the followers of Islam, acted as a judge, and issued regulations for almost every aspect of life—not only for Muslims, but also for non-Muslims who lived under their governance. Unlike Jesus, Muhammad's kingdom was very much of this world. In fact, what he said and did formed the bedrock of the Sharia, the law to be practiced in Muslim countries.

Muhammad and his followers were driven from Mecca to the city of Medina (at that time called Yathrib) in 622 A.D. When they arrived, Muhammad implemented a set of rules to govern the city. This is often called the "Constitution of Medina," although it was hardly the result of voluntary negotiations with the citizens. Muslims like to point out that the twenty-fifth section of that document guarantees religious freedom for non-Muslims. Based on this example, they argue that the *Umma* does not compel anyone's religion. They quote the Quranic verse: "There is no compulsion in religion." [9] But that misses the point, which is that even if the *Umma* does make some allowance for religious minorities to live under theocratic rule, it still seeks to establish itself as an Islamic regime. Its goal is human society governed by Islamic law,

---

[7] Mark 10:35-45.

[8] Sura 3:110.

[9] Qur'an 2:256.

rendering non-Muslims as *dhimmi,* essentially second-class citizens who are subject to Islam and must pay the *jizya* (tax for non-muslims).

Critics of Christianity point out that at times the Church has also sought to control or establish secular kingdoms. In the Middle Ages the dream of "Christendom," which entangled the power of Church and State, produced many abuses. And yet the very fact that Christians acknowledge that these were abuses highlights the difference between the Church of Jesus and the *Umma* of Muhammad. When Pope Leo III placed the crown on Charlemagne's head in Saint Peter's Basilica in 799 A.D. he was doing something that Jesus wouldn't do. Christians themselves have criticized this secularization of the Church ever since.

When Muhammad died in 632, he ruled a religio-political kingdom. The earliest and biggest division in Islam, between the Sunni and Shia branches, arose because of a dispute over who would succeed "the prophet" as the *Amir al-Mu'minin,* or "Commander of the Believers" (another title for caliph). Muhammad's father-in-law, Abu Bakr, won the position, and the Sunni branch of Islam recognizes the Caliphate through his administration. Shiite Muslims wanted to abide by tribal rules and appoint Muhammad's next of kin: his nephew and son-in-law, Ali. But while they disagreed over who should succeed Muhammad, they all agreed that the *Umma* needed a head of state.

Contrast the succession of Muhammad with the weeks following the resurrection of Jesus. Jesus appeared to hundreds of his followers and told them to, "Go and make disciples of all nations, baptizing them in the name of the Father and of the Son and of the Holy Spirit, and teaching them to obey everything I have commanded you. And surely I am with you always, to the very end of the age." [10] Jesus tells them to

---

[10] Matthew 28:18-20.

make disciples from among all nations and to teach them to obey everything which Jesus has commanded, but he doesn't tell them to enforce that legally or militarily. He promises to abide with–and in–his followers, not to establish them into a state.

After all that Jesus taught them, the disciples were still confused about this issue. Consider Jesus' last conversation with his disciples:

> *So when they met together, they asked him, "Lord, are you at this time going to restore the kingdom to Israel?"*
>
> *He said to them: "It is not for you to know the times or dates the Father has set by his own authority. But you will receive power when the Holy Spirit comes on you; and you will be my witnesses in Jerusalem, and in all Judea and Samaria, and to the ends of the earth."*
>
> *After he said this, he was taken up before their very eyes, and a cloud hid him from their sight.* [11]

Jesus never intended to lead a political kingdom, in spite of his disciples' prodding him to do so. Instead of organizing the faithful into an earthly nation, he disappeared into the sky. A short time later, the Kingdom he did come to establish was dispersed among the nations at Pentecost. His apostles scattered as well, and not all of their stories were recorded in the Bible. What happened to Paul or Nathaniel is not important. The Gospel they preached is what matters, and the fruit that it bears. That fruit was evident as my students and I met with the imams in Pretoria. While the *Umma* dreams of conquering the world (as the one imam said), the Church strives to love those in the world who are stumbling in spiritual darkness.

----

[11] Acts 1:6-9.

The *Umma* Grows into Islamic Civilization

When Muhammad died, most of Arabia was under the control of the *Umma*. The first Caliph, Abu Bakr, spent two years fighting the wars of *Ridda* (apostasy) to reconvert tribesmen who had deserted Islam after Muhammad's death. It was left to his successor Umar to expand the lands that fell under the *Umma*'s control. Within his ten-year reign, Muslim armies conquered Iraq and Syria, and had taken Egypt from the Byzantines. From 644-656, Uthman, the third Caliph, conquered northern Africa as far as Libya, occupied all of Persia, and captured the island of Cyprus. Within less than fifty years after Muhammad claimed that Gabriel had begun to reveal the Qur'an to him, the Islamic *Umma* controlled an empire larger than that of Alexander the Great, rivaling the rule of the Caesars at the height of Rome's power.

When Ali became the fourth caliph in 656, the *Umma* experienced its first Sunni-Shiite war. Ali and the Shiites surrendered to the armies of the Syrian Umayyad people, who were Sunnis. This surrender ushered in the beginning of the Umayyad Dynasty, which for almost one hundred years was headquartered in Damascus. The Umayyad caliphs continued the conquest of Islam westwards, sweeping across North Africa until they reached the Atlantic. They also moved into Europe. Between 711 and 713 they took Spain, and between 718 and 720 they invaded France. Their conquest in Europe was only checked in 732, when Charles Martel of France, the grandfather of Charlemagne, halted their advance in the battle of Tours, just over a hundred miles southwest of Paris. In less than a century Islam had conquered the entire Middle East, parts of Europe and Africa, and stretched as far as India and China. In fact, Spain would remain under Muslim control until the Battle of Grenada in 1492. [12]

The Umayyad Dynasty lost control of the Caliphate to the Abbasids, a tribe from the vicinity of Baghdad, in 750. The Abbasids invaded Sicily in 827, took Malta in 869, and conquered the Fatimids of North Africa in 910 and the Buwaihids of Iraq in 945. While Islam remained Arab at its core, it had expanded to become an international religion made up of many non-Arab nations. The rise of the Seljuk Turkish dynasty in the tenth century marked a significant shift in the Caliphate: it was now ruled for the first time by non-Arabs. Turks and Persians, not Arabs, would be the political leaders of the Islamic *Umma* for the next thousand years.

The Islamic Diaspora

Islam spread far beyond Arabia, and the *Umma* eventually included Muslims of many lands and ethnic groups: Kazakhstan on the steppes of Central Asia, the heights of the Hindu Kush in Afghanistan, the coasts of southern Pakistan, the islands of Indonesia, the Atlas Mountains of Morocco, the valleys of southern Spain. Arabs represented only a small percentage of the *Umma*, and they have not been its political leaders since a few centuries after Muhammad. This has led to an internal cultural tension within Islam, as Muslims worldwide kneel facing Mecca in Arabia five times a day, saying prayers in Arabic. Aside from being the home of the *Kaaba*, to which all Muslims must make a pilgrimage at least once in

---

[12] While we do not condone Pope Leo III's coronation of Charlemagne, it should be noted that during the centuries of Islamic conquest, the Church, lacking armies of its own, desperately wanted protection from the expansion of the caliphs. Islam didn't represent just spiritual or religious competition, but a very real military threat. This contributed (along with the temptations of power) to the Church's drift from Jesus' intentions.

their life, Arabia was a backwater of Islamic civilization for twelve centuries. The Arabs have never again achieved the unity and power they had under Muhammad and the first caliphs. To engage Islam was to engage Persians, Turks, or other more influential cultures within the Islamic *Umma*.

The Arabs Return to Power within the *Umma*

In 1917, the Arabs revolted against the Ottoman Turks, who had held the Caliphate for centuries. It was a tumultuous yet pivotal year, with World War I raging in the trenches of France and the Bolshevik Revolution in Russia shuffling the balance of power in Europe, Africa, and the Middle East. The British saw the Arab uprising as an opportunity to open a southeastern front against the Turks, who were allies of Germany in that war. The British supported the Arab insurgency as it took control of Arabia, Syria, and Transjordan from the Turks in 1918. In 1923, Ataturk (the president of Turkey) abolished the Caliphate, and Turkey adopted a secular constitutional government based on a Western model. The Arabs were free from the Turks, and the focus of global politics shifted elsewhere, as the post-WWI colonial powers arbitrarily split them up into neutralized nation-states.

All that changed in 1928, when oil was discovered in Saudi Arabia. Based on ancient tradition, the land belonged neither to the wandering Bedouins nor the merchants of the cities, but to the king–in this case the House of Saud. Suddenly, Arabia mattered very much to the world powers. Suddenly, they had something to export. Suddenly, they were wealthy beyond anything that the caliphs of the seventh and eighth centuries could have possibly imagined.

Saudi wealth has changed Islam in the twentieth century. The Grand Mosque in Mecca, which houses the *Kaaba*, was rebuilt (incidentally by a construction company owned by Osama Bin Laden's father), and Saudi petrodollars have funded the worldwide expansion of one of the most radical sects of Sunni Islam: Wahhabism. Their Shiite rivals in Iran have done the same thing. Oil wealth has built mosques and schools, educated imams, and–in some cases–funded terrorism.

Presently, Islam continues to spread throughout Africa, Asia, the Middle East, and even the secular West. Islamic expansion today uses more sophisticated tools than did the seventh and eight century conquerors. Muslim organizations have been promoting Islam through educational systems, through political activism, and the Internet. However, violence still plays a role: the war against Christians in the north of Nigeria, including the burning of fields and churches, is justified by a seventh-century concept of the *Umma*. The same is true of Sudan, Somalia, and many other Islamic countries.

The *Umma* Today

Most Muslims have deep political convictions arising from their perception that the greater *Umma*, the *Dar Al Islam*, has been humiliated and must be restored. The world wars, colonialism, the breakup of Ottoman Empire, the abolishment of the Caliphate, and the establishment of the state of Israel in 1948–in addition to oil politics, secularization, modernization, tourism, trade, and the proliferation of Western brands and fashion in the heart of ancient Muslim cities–have combined to produce a smoldering anger in Muslim communities around the world. The modern fundamentalist, terrorist, and jihadist movements are all calls to return to the golden age of Islam. Some are even calling for a return to the Caliphate, including Al Qaeda. Indeed, some of his followers and admirers have taken to calling Osama Bin Laden "the Caliph."

The imam in Pretoria, South Africa most probably continues to preach every Friday that Muslims must establish the *Umma* of Islam over the world.

I write these words as I am attending the Third Lausanne Congress on World Evangelization, in Cape Town, South Africa. Four thousand leaders from around the world are here to consider the challenges of the twenty-first century. Naturally, a large number of participants are from African nations. As I mingle among them and hear their hearts and visions, there is one recurring theme: "Muslims are invading our towns and cities," and, "Mosques are being erected everywhere, even in Christian places and no one dares stop them." A number of pastors from various countries in West Africa, East Africa, and Southern Africa have said the exact same thing: "Muslims are moving into leadership positions in education, economics and politics. We feel helpless. What shall we do?"

A pastor made similar remarks in Tatarstan in 2001, as we were standing just outside a huge mosque with eight minarets towering over the city of Kazan. It was intentionally built between the largest Orthodox cathedral and the Kremlin.[13] The pastor said, "Look, Saudi Arabia sent $50 million to build this mosque. See the minarets rising above the steeple and the tower of the Kremlin?" Then with visible pain in his voice he added, "We cannot get enough money to build a small building for our Bible school."

A moment of somber silence followed. I lifted my eyes to the skies and asked for an answer from above. The words of Jesus fell down ringing in my ears, "Tell this brother what I said to my disciples when they seemed worried about earthly things. Tell him not to worry."

I turned to this dear, faithful, hard-working brother who was discouraged by the Islamic "invasion of his nation" and said, "Let us see what Jesus would say. Read Luke 12:32." This was such an encouraging word that what followed was a resolve to persevere and see the world through the eyes of Jesus. Here is what Jesus said to his disciples in that verse, and is say-

---

[13] This is not referring to the famous Moscow Kremlin, but rather the Kazan Kremlin. Kremlin is Russian for "fortress," and is usually the main government building in historic Russian cities.

ing to us today: "Do not be afraid, little flock, for your Father has been pleased to give you the kingdom." [14]

As we see Islam expanding into our cities and neighborhoods, rather than be intimidated, fearful, or angry, let us invite them to the fold of Christ the shepherd, who assured his disciples, "I have other sheep that are not of this sheep pen. I must bring them also. They too will listen to my voice, and there shall be one flock and one shepherd." [15]

And we need to do it one lost sheep at a time.

---

[14] Luke 12:32.
[15] John 10:16.

Chapter 12
Jesus' Model

Commenting on the Parable of the Sower, a missionary speaking at a conference said that it seems some Arab countries are more like a concrete floor than a fertile field. Another missionary leader told me personally that, after four decades of overseeing missionaries in Muslim countries all over the world and using all sorts of strategies and approaches, he has concluded that, "Nothing works, so try anything." He had been discouraged with the lack of fruit in his work. I visited a missionary family in an Arab country where they had been for seven years. When I asked them about their work, he and his wife disclosed: "Frankly, we are discouraged. We have made some friendships but no one has come to the Lord yet." A prominent apologetics ministry has been engaging Muslims in debates and dialogue in mosques for many years. Their reports are full of optimism about the opportunities for further dialogue. I asked one of the staff members, "How many Muslims have you seen come to Christ?" He answered, "We have developed several good relationships." When I pressed him further he admitted that they have not seen one Muslim come to Christ.

Why not? What is the problem? Some say that there is no problem. They refer to famous missionaries who spent decades on the mission field before seeing their first convert. However, when there is no fruit, it is usually blamed on the strategy or the approach.

On the other hand, there are those who report great successes. One ministry has claimed 600,000 followers of Jesus in a Muslim-majority country. Others talk about many churches planted in Muslim lands. At the Lausanne Congress 2010 in

Cape Town, one speaker reported a thousand imams coming to Christ in West Africa.

Happily, there are many who are bearing fruit and there are Muslims coming to Christ. It is sad that some are not. But the big question is: how do we know if what we are doing is *right?* Are results a good indicator of the rightness or wrongness of our methods? Every missiological model claims results. Often these models contradict one another. If both are finding success, does that prove that they are both right? Some say, "Yes, God can use any and all methods." They argue that Paul said he would do anything so that by all means he may save some.[1] But the biblical answer is a resounding "NO!" Neither results nor lack of results proves anything. If results are proof of truth, then Islam is right because there are over a billion Muslims.

A few years ago I attended a conference in Asia with my son Pierre. Various strategies were mentioned, all with encouraging results. As we were lining up for lunch, one missions leader asked me, "What do you think?" I asked him to tell me first what he thought. He replied, "Honestly, I don't know anymore."

Confusion and divisiveness have plagued the missionary movement of our generation. In the last four decades or so, missionaries have been encouraged to come up with innovative methods and approaches. In a postmodern world, standards and absolutes are frowned at and mocked. It sometimes feels like the days of the ancient Israelite Judges, when "everyone did what was right in their own eyes."[2]

What mission agency, church, or individual is providing a model for us as we seek to evangelize Muslims? What book, journal, or magazine contains the proven strategies, methods, and approaches that we can adopt in witnessing to Muslims?

---

[1] 1 Corinthians 9:22.

[2] Judges 17:6, 21:25.

There are many schools of missiology, seminaries, and training programs. There are more books than anyone can read. There are more seminars and conferences than anyone can attend. Strategies, approaches, and models of ministry are too numerous to even keep track of. A.W. Tozer hit the nail on the head with these prophetic words that still ring true:

> *"Right now we are in an age of religious complexity. The simplicity that is in Christ is rarely found among us. In its stead are programs, methods, organizations and a world of nervous activities which occupy time and attention but can never satisfy the longing of the heart. The shallowness of our inner experience, the hollowness of our worship, and that servile imitation of the world which marks our promotional methods all testify that we, this day, know God only imperfectly, and the peace of God scarcely at all."* [3]

There has to be an answer. We cannot go about ministry with a trial and error mentality. Enormous financial and human resources are wasted on experimentation, as missionaries hope to stumble on the secret of success.

On the eve of the Islamic takeover of the Christian Middle East, the Church was consumed by theological debates and heresy. The Bolshevik Revolution occurred while the Orthodox Church was consumed by its internal struggles. Today is no different; Islam is spreading far and wide while we are consumed by methodological debates. Mosques are replacing churches in Europe and new mosques are being erected in huge numbers, even in Christian lands. A paradigm shift is needed for the missionary movement to make an impact on the lost peoples of the world, including Muslims.

---

[3] Aiden W. Tozer, The Pursuit of God, (1957 Camp Hill, PA: Christian Publications), pg. 17.

Jesus is the Answer

We tell sinners that Jesus is the answer to life's problems. Do we believe that he is the answer to our missiological problems too? Jesus left his glory and came down to die on the cross to save us. But he also lived among us, to leave us an example to follow and a model for life and ministry. Numerous times, and in different ways, Jesus instructed his disciples to "learn from me."[4] I would paraphrase Jesus' instructions this way: *"Watch me. See how I treat people of all walks of life. Hear my parables and watch me answer those who oppose me. Follow me to Golgotha and see me on the cross. Think of why I pour out my blood for those I love. Learn from me. Then do exactly what I have done and teach what I have taught you. Train others the way I have trained you. One day I will leave you to do it on your own."*

This sums it all up.

The life of Jesus is the only authoritative standard of ministry. Everything else we read, hear about, or observe is subservient to what Jesus has taught us by his words and deeds.

If Jesus is not the model, then who is? We do not model our ministries after pioneers like Samuel Zwemer, Hudson Taylor, or William Carey. These and many others were great people who have accomplished much for the Kingdom. They sacrificed much. We honor them and we can learn from them, but we do not model our lives after them. We don't need to. The model of Jesus is all we need.

I want to share with you four of the most significant lessons I have learned from the life and ministry of Jesus. Obviously, a short chapter cannot be a comprehensive study of the model of Jesus. But I hope to whet your appetite to dig deeper for yourself, to learn from the Master.

---

[4] Matthew 11:29.

How Jesus Prepared: He Faced-Off with Satan

When I first sensed God's call to minister to Muslims, a veteran missionary warned me, "Ministry to Muslims is like entering a war zone. You will be attacked on every front." As the years went by, these words proved to be correct.

Paul calls Timothy, and others, fellow-soldiers.[5] Every Christian is a soldier in the Lord's army, fighting the good fight.[6] It is a continuous struggle to have victory in our own lives, as well as a struggle on behalf of Muslims who are held captive[7] by Satan's deception.

Soldiers do not go to the front lines of the battle unprepared. They go through rigorous training. When they are physically, mentally, and emotionally fit for the dangerous task, then and only then are they sent to do battle.

At the age of thirty, Jesus was about to begin his public ministry. Well aware of the hardships before him, he took to the desert after his baptism to fast for forty days in preparation for the humanly impossible task ahead. The Logos[8] of God was entering enemy territory to snatch humanity from the claws of death and rescue them from hell. That meant a head-on confrontation with Satan. Our Lord did not shrink back. He willingly went to the desert "to be tested by the devil."[9]

---

[5] 1 Corinthians 9:7; Philippians 2:25; 2 Timothy 2:3,4; Philemon 1:2.

[6] 2 Timothy 4:7.

[7] 2 Timothy 2:26 "that they will come to their senses and escape from the trap of the devil, who has taken them captive to do his will."

[8] Logos is the Greek word for Word. John 1:1"In the beginning was the Word, and the Word was with God, and the Word was God."

[9] Matthew 4:1 "Then Jesus was led by the Spirit into the desert to be tempted by the devil."

Reaching the Muslim world is the greatest challenge facing the Church of Jesus Christ. Not only is it difficult, it is impossible. [10] No amount of knowledge, strategies, or experience can put a dent in the thick wall separating Muslims from Christ. As we purpose to penetrate the Muslim world with the Gospel, our task is no different than that of our Lord. We are entering enemy territory to snatch people from the fire of hell. How are we to do the tasks of Jesus without following in the steps of our Master? As Jesus fasted and prayed to face the enemy, let us take this seriously and take time to fast and pray, pleading with God to fill us with his Spirit and prepare our hearts with faith, courage, and boldness.

The key to the success of our Lord Jesus was the presence of the Holy Spirit in him. Luke made this reality absolutely clear: "Jesus, full of the Holy Spirit, returned from the Jordan and was led by the Spirit in the desert, where for forty days he was tempted by the devil." [11] When he was about to leave the earth, Jesus assured his disciples, "...you will receive power when the Holy Spirit comes on you; and you will be my witnesses in Jerusalem, and in all Judea and Samaria, and to the ends of the earth." [12] This is a promise we need to embrace and seek.

Ministry to Muslims is not for wimps. It requires faith, boldness, courage, and resilience. Humanly, we are all wimps. This is why we desperately need spiritual preparation to go to the battle filled with the Holy Spirit, who gives us the courage

---

[10] Luke 18:27 "What is impossible with men is possible with God."

[11] Luke 4:1,2.

[12] Acts 1:8.

and who fights for us. For the battle is the Lord's. [13] We cannot face the immense challenge of the Muslim world without the presence of the Holy Spirit in our lives.

In recent decades, spiritual requirements have been almost completely missing from missionary recruitment. Thousands of young people go on short term mission trips with little understanding of the spiritual battle that they are getting into. It seems that numbers, budgets, and strategies have become the main foci of our missionary endeavors.

The Apostle John, who was the closest to Jesus, tells us that "The reason the Son of God appeared was to destroy the devil's work." [14] This applies to us, too. Our task is to destroy the devil's work, and we had better not go at it with our might or power, but by the Spirit of God.

When you are on your knees before God, you are declaring war against the devil. When you engage in the ministry of bringing light to darkness, you are declaring a war against the enemy. Those called to evangelize the world are entering into a battle zone. Islam is a stronghold of Satan. Do not go unless you are spiritually prepared.

As we learn the model of Jesus, bear in mind that it is not a method that you can just do to guarantee success. It's not about what you do; it's about what he does through you. You can only bear fruit as the Spirit of God is present in your life and work. You need to be spiritually prepared.

---

[13] 2 Chronicles 20:15 He said: "Listen, King Jehoshaphat and all who live in Judah and Jerusalem! This is what the LORD says to you: 'Do not be afraid or discouraged because of this vast army. For the battle is not yours, but God's.' "

[14] 1 John 3:8.

How Jesus Trained his Team of Disciples

Jesus had only three years to accomplish his task. He therefore focused on choosing and training a few faithful men, and entrusting them with the broader task of making disciples of all nations. His team was his priority. For three years, he invested in them and taught them how to minister to people. He took them with him everywhere, particularly Peter, John, and James.

When Jesus evangelized, he did it with his disciples present, and he often did discipleship with the crowds present. The Sermon on the Mount is a great example. As the crowds gathered, the disciples sat around him, watching everything he did and hearing every word he spoke. [15]

In the early stages of training his disciples, Jesus sent out the twelve by themselves and gave them very clear instructions. Check out Matthew 10 and Luke 9 and 10. See how rigorous and how drastically different the curriculum Jesus used is from our training programs? Shouldn't we be learning how to train our missionary candidates from the Master?

My first introduction to the type of ministry that Jesus carried out was in the mid-sixties, when a team from Operation Mobilization came to Lebanon. I joined OM teams in Lebanon every summer for many years. Leaders went with their teams and witnessed to people door-to-door and in the market place. It began with the founder of OM, George Verwer, [16] a fiery, wiry preacher whose life demonstrated the

---

[15] "Now when he saw the crowds, he went up on a mountainside and sat down. His disciples came to him, and he began to teach them" Matthew 5:1, 2.

[16] George Verwer is an American who founded Operation Mobilization in the late 1950's. He has lived in Britain most of his life. He has made a great impact on me, and I consider him one of the most influential leaders in my life.

servant leadership he learned from his Master. George carried a literature bag and went out knocking on doors like the rest of us. The other OM leaders saw his example and did the same. They went along with their teammates, practicing what they had seen modeled in their leader. Where is this model practiced today? Thank God it exists, although unfortunately it is rare.

This is why many of our *Engaging Islam*[17] training programs include role-plays and mentored ministry. We take people to the streets and parks to meet Muslims and practice what they have learned in class. True discipleship and training are best done in the context of ordinary life, not just from podiums in classrooms and behind closed doors. Training is best done in the public arena. This is the way Jesus did it, and this is the way we must do it.

After a rigorous training program, Jesus passed the vision and responsibility on to them. He commissioned them to go to all the nations and preach the Gospel. But they were not ready to take on the world until they received the power of the Holy Spirit. From then on, the Church was unstoppable.

How Jesus Ministered to Others

Teaching, preaching, and healing: this was the threefold ministry of our Lord Jesus. "Jesus went throughout Galilee, teaching in their synagogues, preaching the good news of the kingdom, and healing every disease and sickness among the people."[18]

As we observe Jesus' pattern, do we see him specializing in only one of these three ministries? Today, we place a high value on specialization in education and practice. You will find certain mission groups involved in medical missions. Others

---

[17] http://engagingislam.org.

[18] Matthew 4:23; 9:35-38.

focus on humanitarian aid. Some are dedicated solely to prayer. There are ministries which do nothing but training, and still others emphasize either evangelism or discipleship.

Following in the steps of Jesus necessitates that we be involved in all three ministries simultaneously. Stephen was the type of man that the church chose to serve tables. [19] Yet we do not see him limiting his work to feeding the needy. He boldly preached the Gospel.

This week I had a Skype meeting with a convert from an Arab country. After an hour of Bible study on various topics, he asked, "How can we help new converts live the new life in Christ?" The missionary who led this man to Christ told me that, "Fifty-five Muslims accepted Christ in the last year, but only two of them are now continuing."

Jesus commissioned us not to just evangelize but to also make disciples of all the nations. He commanded us to teach "them to obey all I have commanded you." [20]

When I visited Northern Iraq to work with the Kurds [21] in the early nineties I stayed with a missionary who introduced me to his first Kurdish convert. I noticed that my host just hung out with Dolovan and talked with him about all kinds of things, but did not study the Bible with him. His idea of discipleship was to just let the convert become part of the family and come in and out as he pleased. In later years I discovered that this mentality was quite common among missionaries.

---

[19] In Acts 6:1-8, Stephen's qualities listed were: full of the Spirit and wisdom (v3), full of faith and of the Holy Spirit (v5), full of God's grace and power, did great wonders and miraculous signs among the people (v8). He was also a preacher (Acts 7).

[20] Matthew 28:20.

[21] I had been working in Kurdistan since 1973 when I began a Bible translation project in the Sorani dialect of Kurdish. The International Bible society (now Biblica) continued the work from the 1990 till the present.

Providing hospitality to the people we work with, and giving them the feeling that they belong to a new family has great value. But unless we also give them the nourishment that they need to grow, they will remain spiritually dwarfed or be perpetually immature. Too many converts have come and gone because they do not get the nourishment they need.

Jesus did not just evangelize. He taught. "After Jesus had finished instructing his twelve disciples, he went on from there to teach and preach in the towns of Galilee." [22] Of course he had previously evangelized his disciples, when he called them to follow him. But that was just the beginning of the relationship: he spent the rest of his time teaching them. The disciples called him teacher. Jesus was intentional in his role as a teacher and his disciples intentionally sat at his feet.

I know a man who has spent years going into the streets to talk to Muslims. When they were ripe he would pray with them and lead them to a relationship with Christ. When I asked him years later where all these people are now, he said they are everywhere. He specialized in evangelism. He was good at it. But without follow up, it was like bearing children and letting them die from malnourishment. Discipleship is like nursing and feeding a newborn baby.

Ideally, every missionary would be like Jesus, who was an evangelist, discipler, *and* trainer. We should strive to have all three of these elements in our ministries. Of course, we each have different gifts, and it's not wrong to specialize to some degree. But having a gift in one area does not exempt you from serving in others. Just because you're good at evangelism, it does not mean that you don't have to take responsibility to see that the people you lead to Christ get good, solid discipleship. You could bring in another person who is gifted in discipleship to help you with this task, but your role does not in-

---

[22] Matthew 11:1.

stantly end once you introduce the two. In many cases like this, the new believer's connection with the one who led them to Christ cannot just be transferred to some other person.

It is your responsibility to see that the people you lead to Christ are nurtured and not just left alone for their new faith to wither and die. Sadly, this is what happens most of the time. Many who have dramatic testimonies have ended up backsliding or becoming perpetually immature.

At a state-wide missionary conference in Alaska where I was speaking, a pastor gave this amazing insight, which I will never forget: "As Jesus was looking at the crowds, he saw harvesters from among the harvest." Since then, I see in every Muslim that I meet the potential to be a future worker in the Kingdom.

The third part of the threefold ministry of Jesus is healing. In the last fifty years the missionary movement has shifted its attention from the soul to the body. The social gospel began being preached, and in five decades the pendulum has swung completely to the opposite extreme. Rather than caring for the body as well as the soul, many now seem to care solely for the body.

The model of Jesus, if followed, will drive us to do all three ministries simultaneously. There is no biblical justification for a humanitarian ministry void of preaching of the Gospel, teaching, and training.

George Verwer wrote a short book called *Revolution of Balance*. [23] Balance is what we need in so many areas of our lives, in our diets, in our work load, and also in our ministry. Jesus balanced care for the soul with care of the body.

---

[23] It was later combined with another book to form "Revolution of Love and Balance." (Walterick Publishers, 1977).

How Jesus Suffered

If you knew that if you went to the mission field a terrorist organization would be looking for you to kill you, would you still go?

When Jesus entered the world, his life was full of danger. Throughout his ministry he faced extreme opposition. The gospels record numerous times when the Pharisees were looking for him to kill him. [24]

The first time that I was invited to deliver talks to a Muslim audience at a theater in Kazan, Tatarstan, the theater owner received bomb threats. The organizers told me that the lectures on Muhammad and Jesus had to be cancelled. The news upset me and frankly frightened me, a little. At three o'clock in the morning a horrible nightmare jolted me out of bed, shaking and sweating. I dreamed that I walked down the aisle of the theater to give my speech, but when I opened my bag to get out my Bible, my severed head was inside, dripping with blood. For over an hour I sought the Lord as to whether this nightmare was from him or the enemy. Reading through the first thirty-four Psalms assured me that fear was not from God and that the Lord is in control. "The Lord is my light and my salvation, whom shall I fear?" [25] I praise God that the leaders decided to find another venue and hundreds crowded the newly found theater. It was glorious. The theater was so packed that I asked the Christians in attendance to give up their seats for Muslims. They huddled in the lobby and prayed, and after two nights of lectures I returned home unscathed. At those two meetings, fifty Muslims signed up to study the Bible with local believers, including an imam.

---

[24] Luke 19:47 "Every day he was teaching at the temple. But the chief priests, the teachers of the law and the leaders among the people were trying to kill him."

[25] Psalm 27:1.

From the start, Jesus did not hide from his disciples the fact that following him could bring persecution upon them. He told them, "Blessed are you when people insult you, persecute you and falsely say all kinds of evil against you because of me." [26]

Much later his message was still the same. "...they will lay hands on you and persecute you. They will deliver you to synagogues and prisons, and you will be brought before kings and governors, and all on account of my name." [27]

When Jesus called Saul on the road to Damascus he did not hide from him the suffering he was going to face. Jesus instructed Ananias in a vision, "Go! This man (Saul, later called Paul) is my chosen instrument to carry my name before the Gentiles and their kings and before the people of Israel. I will show him how much he must suffer for my name." [28]

When we understand our calling, we can withstand any trial or tribulation because it is what we signed up for. But if we hide this element from new converts, they will feel cheated. They expect joy and peace in the new life and instead they get trouble and persecution. I have met a number of Christians from Muslim Backgrounds who are ready to die for Christ because they understood the full truth of what the Gospel is all about. But then again I have met those who are wimps. Whenever they face any difficulty, even if it is mild, they collapse. The truth is that when Jesus offers us life he bids us to die. He said, "Whoever finds his life will lose it, and whoever loses his life for my sake will find it." [29]

---

[26] Matthew 5:11.

[27] Luke 21:12.

[28] Acts 9:15-16.

[29] Matthew 10:39.

Suffering is part and parcel of the Gospel. Early on we must warn people that they are exchanging the earthly with the heavenly. They must learn that following Jesus means carrying the cross daily.

The first time I heard George Verwer, he spoke on, "Forsaking All, I Follow Him." [30] He demonstrated from the gospels that Jesus calls us to deny ourselves, carry the cross, and die to ourselves and the world. A life in Christ is a life of total abandonment. [31] It is this to which we are calling Muslims, and any other people. I have not heard this preached upon in missions conferences for many years. Instead, the emphasis during the last three decades has been on cultural adjustment rather than on the transforming power of the Gospel.

Today, the Gospel message is so watered down that people think they are coming to Christianity just to be free from legalism, sin, and guilt. This is not the complete Gospel. It is only half the story. God's call is a heavenly calling. Paul understood this life well when he said, "For me to live is Christ and to die is gain," [32] and, "He died for all, that those who live should no longer live for themselves but for him who died for them and was raised again." [33]

Peter makes it clear that we must emulate Christ in his suffering. "To this you were called, because Christ suffered for you, leaving you an example, that you should follow in his steps...When they hurled their insults at him, he did not re-

---

[30] This topic is covered in his book, *Out of the Comfort Zone* (George Verwer, Bethany House Publishers, 2001).

[31] Total Abandon is a book written by the husband of a martyred nurse in Lebanon. Gary Witherall, *Total Abandon* (Tyndale House Publishers, Inc., 2005).

[32] Philippians 1:21.

[33] 2 Corinthians 5:15.

taliate; when he suffered, he made no threats. Instead, he entrusted himself to him who judges justly." [34]

The blood of the martyrs has been, and will continue to be, the seed of the Church. [35] In the culmination of all things we read these dramatic words: "They overcame him by the blood of the Lamb and by the word of their testimony; they did not love their lives so much as to shrink from death." [36]

Our Lord Jesus lived the perfect life. His lifestyle and ministry are the ultimate standard for us to follow. He was intentional in training and preparing his team for a humanly impossible task. Yet with his life he demonstrated how we must minister to others. Jesus never asked the apostles to do anything that he was not willing to do himself. He was the pacesetter and the coach. The Apostle Paul followed the example of Jesus when he said, "And the things you have heard me say in the presence of many witnesses entrust to reliable men who will also be qualified to teach others." [37] What he was really saying here is, "Pass it on to those who will pass it on."

Following Christ is not a theory or a romantic idea. It is a journey of faith through life's sufferings on behalf of Christ, all the way to Calvary.

[34] I Peter 2:21-22.

[35] Tertullian (circa 160-circa 220 A.D.) wrote "the blood of the martyrs is the seed of the Church" in a treatise called *Apologeticus*.

[36] Revelation 12:11.

[37] 2 Timothy 2:2.

Chapter 13
Love as Jesus Loved

All eyes were on Jesus as he stood before the tomb of Lazarus.[1] The Jews were wondering what he would do. "Could not he who opened the eyes of the blind man have kept this man from dying?" They had seen Jesus perform all sorts of miracles, many times. Why did he not heal Lazarus before he died? Mary and Martha wondered the same thing, and felt the same emotions. They told him, "Lord, if you had been here, my brother would not have died." No one imagined that Jesus could do anything for Lazarus once he had been dead for days. How did Jesus feel about this lack of faith? He who knows the contents of all hearts knew that humans look at the gift rather than the giver, the miracle rather than the miracle worker. Moved with compassion, he wept.

His tears altered the tone of the drama between Jesus and those around him. They no longer saw Jesus as just a miracle worker. As he stood there weeping, this powerful man with supernatural powers now appeared so human, so vulnerable, so real, and so genuine. They were amazed, and exclaimed, "See how he loved him!"

Love: nothing else is the heart of God and the heart of the Gospel. Everything we do must stem from love. We love because he is love and his love has reached down to the depths of darkness to pull us out into the bright light.

Does Jesus love all Muslims? Did he die for them? No doubt your answer is an emphatic, "Yes, of course!" Perhaps the verse, "For God so loved the world that he gave his only

---

[1] John 11, various verses used.

son"[2] pops into your head. We all agree that Jesus' life on earth was characterized by love. In the three years of his ministry, our Lord touched the untouchables, reached out to children and women, and healed lepers and outcasts. He loved the poor and the weak: Jews, Samaritans, and Greeks alike. Even the adulterous and demon-possessed found love in him. In him the sick found healing, the bereaved found comfort, and the dead found life. This is the kind of love we need in our lives, particularly as we reach out to those outside the faith.

The gospels record many stories where the word "love" is specifically used to express the relationship Jesus had with people. Here are three examples:

- Jesus loved Lazarus so much that he wept at his tomb. [3]

- Jesus loved the rich young ruler and cared to answer his questions. [4]

- Jesus loved the tax collectors and sinners and invested his life in them. [5]

The love of Jesus was irresistible. People gravitated to him. In fact, they came to him in such large numbers that sometimes Jesus had to hide from crowds to rest.

Six Types of People Came to Jesus

Jesus loved everyone, regardless of who they were. A cross-sectional view of the crowds reveals six types of people that interacted with him, and not all of them had pure motives:

---

[2] John 3:16.

[3] John 11:36.

[4] Mark 10:21.

[5] Luke 7:34.

- *Opportunists:* Those who came because they wanted to benefit from Jesus, especially when he was offering a free meal. He loved them enough to serve them anyway.

- *Spectators:* Those who were intrigued by his miracles and teachings, and were curious to see a good show. He loved them and included them anyway.

- *Seekers:* Those who were hungry and thirsty for righteousness. He loved them and satisfied their needs by teaching them.

- *Outsiders:* Samaritans, tax collectors, women with bad reputations, and lepers. People disliked by Jews and others were loved and welcomed by Jesus.

- *The Needy:* The sick, children, and the poor. He loved them and ministered to them.

- *Critics and Enemies:* These were the Jewish leaders, the Pharisees, Sadducees, and scribes. He loved them enough to confront them with the truth.

It was the love of Jesus that drew the masses to him. They followed him everywhere he went. Love has a magnetic quality that draws people to us. Our love earns us respect and trust. Our love is a witness in itself because it reflects the love of Christ. Our love for others opens doors for us to share the Gospel.

Telling the Truth in Love

When I was in college, I watched a short educational film of a young woman performing as an actor in a stage play. She was a rather obviously bad actor; she did not remember all her lines, she tripped a couple of times, and her voice was barely audible. During the intermission she ran excitedly to her fiancé and asked him, "What do you think? How did I do?" The film stopped at that point and the students in my class were asked, "How would you answer if you were the fiancé?"

Some of my classmates thought that the fiancé should not tell the truth because that could hurt her and damage his relationship with her. They concluded it would be better to encourage her by finding something positive in her performance to praise. Others said that it would be dishonest to give the actor the wrong impression because not telling her the truth would deny her the opportunity to face her weaknesses and try to improve.

The missionary movement is divided by a similar dilemma. Should we confront Muslims point blank and expose their false religion? Or should we be peaceable and find common ground? Again, the life of Jesus provides the answer.

The Two Faces of Love

Most of us like to picture Jesus as gentle, kind, and soft-hearted, and he certainly was all those things. But there was another side of Jesus' personality that most of us don't like to think about: he was confrontational and rude–even displaying anger and physical violence at the Temple. But did that make him any less loving? Jesus loved perfectly, like no one else can love, yet he confronted people with the truth for their own good.

People usually choose one of the two faces of love: grace or judgement. But Jesus' love was multidimensional. To love like Jesus loved we must balance our grace with truth and our truth with grace.

How Jesus Loved the Samaritan Woman

Listen to how Jesus loved the Samaritan woman, yet confronted her with the truth: "You Samaritans worship what you do not know; we worship what we do know, for salvation is from the Jews." [6] But wasn't this an insult to her Samaritan religion? Can you, in fact, get yourself to say to a Muslim, "You Muslims worship what you do not know; we Christians worship what we do know, for salvation is from the Christians"?

Notice how the Samaritan woman's heart melted when she was confronted with the truth. In my experience, whenever I have told Muslims the truth, they appreciated it and responded positively. People of the Middle East appreciate direct speech because they are tired of smooth but dishonest words.

Once I was witnessing to a retired imam from Iraq. I asked him, "Are you sure you will go to heaven if you die today?"

"No one can be sure," answered Imam Hassan.

I tried another approach. "Do you have insurance on your car?"

Imam Hassan looked puzzled. "Of course I do, why?"

"Are you current on your payments? Is your insurance policy in effect?"

"Yes, I pay all my bills," he answered, slightly taken aback that I would suggest otherwise.

"So if you–God forbid–get into an accident, will the insurance company cover it?"

Imam Hassan was now very curious as to where I was going with this line of reasoning. "Why, yes. Certainly."

I smiled, hoping that he would see the love that compelled me to make this next point. "Forgive me for saying this, but it seems to me that your insurance company is more trustworthy than your religion."

Imam Hassan paused for a few seconds. Then he crossed his arms. Finally he admitted, "You are right."

He went on to confess that he had been listening to Arabic Christian radio for four years. The conversation took a turn in

---

[6] John 4:22.

the right direction, and within an hour he was ready to accept Christ as his savior.

I call these moments "divine appointments." He was ripe. He just needed a nudge. I was in the right place at the right time.

Confrontation does not always work. Many whom Jesus confronted were angry and plotted to kill him. Our guiding principle is to do everything in love.

How Jesus Loved Nicodemus

Nicodemus was not just *any* man. He was a leading Pharisee, and a respected expert on the Old Testament. He practiced the Mosaic laws and revered God. When he came to Jesus he began the conversation by flattering Jesus, perhaps trying to "butter him up." Yet Jesus broke into his heart, through the veneer of his religious piety, with a shockingly confrontational assertion: "You must be born again or you will not see the kingdom of God." [7] Wasn't that an insensitive and confusing approach to a man who held such a high position as a teacher of the Jews? Shouldn't Jesus have shown more respect and consideration of Nicodemus' station and context?

At least two imams attended my lecture comparing Muhammad with Jesus in Tatarstan in 2007. When the time came for questions, one red-bearded imam blurted out, "We cannot trust the Bible. It has been corrupted." He was sitting in the front row. I could have answered him with all the arguments I knew about the reliability of the Bible. Often I have chosen to do just that. But the Spirit of God prompted me to point at him and rebuke him. "Shame on you for accusing God of being too weak to protect his word and allowing mere men to corrupt his word," I said. "Right now, repent from this grievous sin."

---

[7] John 3:1-7.

Silence fell on the auditorium for two seconds and the imam, startled by my rebuke, shouted, "1 am sorry, sorry!" 1 went on to respond to questions by the audience, and he did not open his mouth again. Fortunately, 1 had a chance to talk with him after the event, and he stayed around talking to me and other Christians until midnight. When we speak with the loving authority Jesus gave us, people are shaken and awakened.

How Jesus Loved the Rich Young Ruler

Mark wrote in his gospel that, "Jesus looked at him and loved him. 'One thing you lack,' he said. 'Go, sell everything you have and give to the poor, and you will have treasure in heaven. Then come, follow me.' " [8] Didn't Jesus know that this man had spent a lifetime building his wealth? Asking him to give up everything was cruel and unreasonable. It would rock his world, shake his entire lifestyle, destabilize his family, and expose him to unreasonable hardships. To a Western reader, Christ's challenge to this man was hard enough. But an Eastern reader recognizes immediately that selling all his possessions and giving them to the poor would not be just a loss of personal finances, but also a rejection and betrayal of his entire extended-family community, who relied on the resources of this young ruler for its livelihood, status, and future. It wasn't just his future at stake. Remember also that this man was religious. He had memorized and observed the law. Yet Jesus was not impressed by his devotion. Jesus did not hesitate to ask him to choose between following Christ and the world. This was the embodiment of tough–but true–love.

Jesus loved people like the Samaritan woman, Nicodemus, and the rich young ruler enough to confront them with life-changing truth. Jesus did not give them just a touchy-feely, sentimental kind of love. He told them the truth–hard, neces-

---

[8] Mark 10:21.

sary truth–in love. Jesus said that he did not come for the healthy but for the sick. [9] He came to seek and save the lost. [10] He was in the business of changing lives radically (that is, "from the root" [11]).

How Jesus Loved the Pharisees

Jesus loved the Pharisees, Sadducees, scribes, and teachers of the law, and yet he was unrelenting in his attacks on these Jewish leaders. He hurled insults and woes on them, to their face and in the presence of the crowds. Matthew 23 is not an account of a gentle approach toward the Pharisees and teachers of the law. Jesus:

- Exposed their secret ungodly motives (verses 1-7).

- Called them hypocrites (verse 13).

- Told them "woe to you" ten times in this chapter alone.

- Called them "son[s] of hell" (verse 15).

- Called them blind guides and blind fools (verses 16-17).

- Called them "whitewashed tombs" (verse 27).

- Told them, "you are full of hypocrisy and wickedness" (verse 28).

- Called them a brood of vipers and snakes (verse 33).

- Judged them as murderers of the righteous (verses 35-37).

- Did not accept their claim to belong to Abraham (John 8:39).

---

[9] Luke 5:31.

[10] Luke 19:10.

[11] The word "radical" comes from the Latin *radicalis*, which means "from the root."

- Accused them of being children of the devil (John 8:44).

Jesus did not stop there. He also warned the public about them: "Be careful. Be on your guard against the yeast of the Pharisees and Sadducees and against their teaching."[12] What kind of love is this? This sounds more like hate than love, doesn't it?

Those involved in polemic and apologetic ministries use the example of Jesus as the rationale for their confrontational approach. After much thought and prayer about this, I discovered something about Jesus. There are two ways we can learn from him: through his example, and through his commands. There is no question that we must obey his commands. However, there are some things *he* did that he didn't command *us* to do. In these cases we must be careful not to overstep our boundaries. For example, Jesus has the authority and the right to judge, but we do not. The Bible is clear that judgement is God's job, not ours: "It is mine to avenge; I will repay."[13]

He specifically told the disciples what to do in many situations. But he did not tell them what to do with the Pharisee-type. He told us to preach, teach, and heal, but he did not instruct us to attack anyone. We must follow the Holy Spirit's guidance to know when to preach judgement, and when to demonstrate God's grace. But whether your style is polemic (confrontational), apologetic (defending the faith), irenic (peaceful dialogue) or kerygmatic (proclamation), you must love as Jesus loved. Peter admonishes, "Always be prepared to give an answer to everyone who asks you to give the reason for the hope that you have. But do this with gentleness and respect."[14]

---

[12] Matthew 16:6,12.

[13] Deuteronomy 32:35, Romans 12:19, Hebrews 10:30.

[14] 1 Peter 3:15.

Love Your Enemies

In case you are wondering whether the way Jesus treated his opponents was really loving or not, remember what he taught us: "But love your enemies, do good to them, and lend to them without expecting to get anything back. Then your reward will be great, and you will be sons of the Most High, because he is kind to the ungrateful and wicked." [15]

Yousef from North Africa was given a tract in which he read, "Love your enemies." He could not believe his own eyes when he read these strange words. They were so against the grain of his own thinking that he resented them. But he was curious who would write such a crazy thing. That led him to read the New Testament, and that led him to Christ.

Maha from Egypt left Islam, became a communist and found both void of love. When she finally read the Gospel of John, it was the loving compassion of Jesus that drew her to him. The way he dealt with the adulterous woman was beyond anything she had ever experienced growing up in a Muslim home. Islam's solution to sin is ruthless punishment, but Christ's answer is tender loving grace, filled with truth and challenge. This is the distinguishing mark of the Christian.

Loving our enemies is the utmost expression of love. Jesus hung on the cross with his arms stretched out and cried, "Father, forgive them, for they do not know what they are doing." [16]

I have struggled to love my enemies. As a Lebanese Christian I have seen what Muslims have done to Christians throughout history. From childhood I was fed hatred toward Muslims, and without the Spirit's intervention it would have consumed me. But by grace the Lord has given me a love for all Muslim peoples of the world. Amazingly, Jesus considers

---

[15] Luke 6:35.

[16] Luke 23:34.

loving the our enemies as evidence that we are sons of God. He no doubt is referring to God's character of love and that his children have the same character.

Wholistic Ministry [17]

Perhaps the clearest teaching of Jesus on wholistic ministry is in the parable of the sheep and the goats in Matthew 25:31-46. If we were to derive a theology of salvation from this passage only, we would conclude that going to heaven or hell really depends on whether we care for the physical needs of poor strangers. Of course, this is not Christ's intention here. But it is rather sobering to imagine that our eternal destiny could depend on how we treat the needy. Jesus puts it both in the positive and negative. Those who have a wholistic ministry are told, "Come, you who are blessed by my Father; take your inheritance, the kingdom prepared for you since the creation of the world."

On the other side are those whose hearts were cold toward those who were hungry, thirsty, strangers, naked, sick, or in prison. These will hear, "Depart from me, you who are cursed, into the eternal fire prepared for the devil and his angels." Then comes this frightening sentence: "Then they will go away to eternal punishment, but the righteous to eternal life." Jesus really takes it personally when we care, or don't care for the whole person.

How do we theologically understand this teaching? Jesus is basically saying that a compassionate ministry is evidence of our salvation. This is why he was hard on the hypocrites. They believed something that had no impact on their lifestyle. Rather than caring for people, they abused them; rather than including people they rejected them.

---

[17] The modern spelling of this word is "holistic." I prefer the old spelling because it emphasizes the whole of man, which is the purpose of this discussion.

Love as Jesus Loved

No one ever loved as Jesus loved. "Greater love has no one than this, that he lay down his life for his friends." [18] The love of Jesus was not in words; he loved to the last drop of his blood. How then can we explain his attack on the Jewish leaders?

The answer is really not that complicated. Jesus loved each person in a different way. He spoke the love languages that his audience *needed* to hear, although often that was not what they *wanted* to hear. To some, his love was a tough love that shook his audience and confronted them with their sin. A grace-oriented message to the Pharisees would be an endorsement of their hypocrisy. A harsh approach to the woman caught in adultery would be a judgement against someone who already felt judged. We need discernment of the Spirit of God to know when to be gentle and when to be tough, when to convict people of sin, and when to reveal God's forgiveness to them.

How Do We Love Muslims the Way Jesus Loves?

Jesus called all people to repentance, which means making a change of direction. Tough love may require shaking certain Muslims up, awakening them out of the lie they live in and the false teaching they believe in. To accept Muslims as they are may well be the most unloving thing you could do. In my experience, when I have lovingly confronted Muslims I have found them appreciative and responsive. A man from Saudi Arabia begged me to tell him what I thought of Muhammad. I often try to dodge the question, but this time I saw his sincerity and I told him outright that Muhammad is a false prophet and that Jesus predicted him. I sensed a deep relief in him, and

---

[18] John 15:13.

he said, "I have been suspecting that myself for a long time." People are looking for guidance from those in the know. If you are viewed as one who knows, do not deny people the truth.

Loving a Muslim often means creating a conflict in their mind and heart to force them to consider the claims of Christ that contradict their worldview. No one will change without experiencing deeply felt conflicts. I often tell Muslims, "If Islam is not from God, it is not your fault. You were born into it. But it would be your fault if you accept what you have been taught blindly and you do not search for the truth."

We must create spiritual conflicts for those who are slumbering in the comfort zone of their religious beliefs and practices. This is what Jesus did. And this is what Jesus wants to do through us as we engage Muslims. His goal is to transform them into his likeness by calling them out of their miserable darkness into his glorious kingdom of light. A Gospel that does not shake people up and turn them upside down is not the Gospel of Jesus.

Muslims everywhere are looking for rescue. They may initially resist your efforts. But if they see that your motivation is genuine concern–to snatch them out of the fire of hell–they are likely to respond positively. Who, on his way to hell, would not appreciate you standing in their way and saying to them, "STOP! Don't go there! Please, turn around and live!"?

This is how we love the way that Jesus loved.

Chapter 14
Love in Action

Love, love, love. It's all about love.

The first time I shared the Gospel with a Muslim, it was against my will. As I described in the introduction to this book, I was pressured by Ulrich Bruderer, a Swiss missionary in Lebanon. He asked me to join his Operation Mobilization team and go door-to-door in a Muslim village. When I objected he asked me, "Didn't Jesus die for Muslims too?"

"Well, uh..." I stumbled. "I did not think of this before."

Ulrich turned my life around with his reply. "Georges, God so loved the WORLD–not just the Christians of the world. Isn't that right?"

I could not argue with him. Confused and unsure of myself, I went along. It did not take long for God to begin working on my heart. It happened in the very first house we visited. A young man opened the door and invited us in. He provided lavish hospitality, with fruits, cookies, and juices. As I looked at this young man, the Lord planted a seed of love in my heart for him and his people, the Muslims of the world. I was fourteen years old.

You may be engaging a Muslim using the most proven theories, strategies, and approaches. Yet without love, your witness is like "a resounding gong or a clanging cymbal." [1] Everything we say and do must be bathed in love. This is the way of the Master. This must be our way too. Engaging Muslims is about loving them into the Kingdom. We must see them as people for whom Jesus died because of his great love for them.

---

[1] 1 Corinthians 13:1.

How Can We Love Muslims?

Engaging Muslims on a personal level–up close and face-to-face–can be both difficult and easy. The most difficult part is the first step you take toward developing a relationship with your Muslim neighbor, friend, colleague, classmate, boss, employee, or just the man or woman you meet in the marketplace.

When I was a teenager, a visiting pastor taught on 1 Thessalonians 1:3, in which Paul praises the church for their labor of love. The pastor stressed that love is labor, work, and action. The words that still ring in my ears, forty-five years later are these: "If you love someone, take a step toward him." I did not think too much about it until the next day when I met someone on the street that I had never reached out to, although I had known him since I was a child. He was on the "other side." The pastor's words–"If you love someone take a step toward him"–popped into my mind. I did not like the guy and I really did not want to associate with him. But God would not allow me to keep my heart closed any longer. I crossed the road and greeted him. The rest is history. We developed a close friendship that resulted in his coming to Christ, going to seminary years later, and becoming a minister of the Gospel.

Love is Still the Attraction

Between 2005 and 2008, I took on the challenge of surveying as many Muslim converts to Christianity as I could find in the USA. I prepared a questionnaire with 12 questions and gave it to over 120 people at various conferences. The vast majority of Christians from Muslim backgrounds expressed that the love of Christians was a major factor in drawing them to Christ. In my interviews with them, some had fond memories of Christians reaching out to them in love. This survey was just one small confirmation of the importance of love.

After years of ministry around the world, my wife and I accepted the challenge of reaching international students in Boulder, Colorado. To prepare for this type of work I read a paper written by Dr. Everett Boyce. [2] He had interviewed seventeen Indonesian converts from Islam in an effort to discover the major factors that led to their conversion. It should not come as any surprise that one hundred percent of them were attracted by the love that Christians showed them. Those interviews were conducted in the 1970s.

In 2008, I was the host of a TV program directed toward an Arab audience. Before the program started, one of the three guests I had invited on the program made a comment to the effect that he was going to provoke Muslims by attacking the character of their prophet, Muhammad. As gently as I could, I told him and the others that as long as I was the host of the program the dominant theme would be love. I asked each one of them to prepare to give the viewers a one-minute message at the very start of the program. Each was supposed to look straight into the camera and tell the Muslims watching that he loved them. They did, and the atmosphere of the program was good and positive. Many Muslims called, asking specific questions rather than fighting and arguing. After the ninety-minute program ended, one of the guests said, "This was really good. We were able to share the love of Christ."

Without love, the truth cannot be expressed appropriately. Wasn't it the love of Jesus that attracted us to him? I was only eleven when I heard of God's love from a Baptist preacher. After quoting John 3:16 [3] he told me, "Georges, God loves you so

---

[2] Everett Boyce was vice-president of International Students Incorporated. Later in the 1990's he became co-founder of InterFACE Ministries with Bob Culver, based in Atlanta, Georgia.

[3] John 3:16 "For God so loved the world that he gave his one and only Son, that whoever believes in him shall not perish but have eternal life."

much that even if you were the only one on earth he would leave the glory of heaven and come down to die for you." That blew me away. I could not fathom God's love in light of my sin and the dark direction my life was taking. That set me off onto a journey, seeking to know God and his love. A year later, during an evangelistic evening service at my small church in Tripoli, the fiery preacher Maurice Gerges, [4] spoke of the love of God with such passion that I was not able to resist God's love any longer. When he spoke about Christ's suffering on the cross I was sweating as if I had just walked out of a steam room. It was God's love, the compassionate heart of Jesus that put me under such "hot" conviction. That night I surrendered to God and accepted Christ as my loving savior. Two years later, with the help of my mentor, Ulrich, God began to place the burden of loving Muslims into the Kingdom onto my heart.

At a conference for Christians from Muslim Backgrounds, I asked the eighty people in attendance to share the one verse that impacted them the most. One fourth of those present raised their hands, twenty men and women who had left Islam because of the love of God. One Pakistani woman stood up and turned to the audience and, with a poetic style, passionately recited the verse. As she began to say out loud, "God so loved the world...," smiles, amens and hallelujah's echoed through the meeting hall. She had touched a chord in many hearts.

But it is easier said than done. It is easy to love in word, but we all struggle to love in deed. The Apostle John, the beloved disciple of Jesus, prods us with these endearing words:

---

[4] Maurice Gerges is a Lebanese evangelist who has been called the Billy Graham of the Middle East. Thousands in Egypt, Jordan, Syria, Lebanon, and elsewhere have been saved through his ministry. He is retired in California, although he still does some preaching.

"Dear children, let us not love with words or tongue but with actions and in truth." [5]

Debating the Imam in Love

In the mid-1990s I accepted an invitation to debate an imam at the University of Denver. InterVarsity Christian Fellowship had accepted the challenge by the imam to find a Christian leader who would agree to debate him. For the first forty-five minutes the imam launched an attack on the Bible, alleging that it has been corrupted. When my turn came, the atmosphere was electric. More than six hundred Muslims in attendance paid careful attention to me when I stood up to speak. I could tell that they expected me to launch a counterattack. And, as you may expect, they were all ready to "boo" me as I have seen them do on some other occasions.

I decided not to fall into that trap. Instead, I stood up and said, "As a young man, I hated Muslims with a passion! I hated Muslims for all they had done to my family and my country." I shared stories of the war that I lived through for several years in Lebanon. I told them how my house was destroyed, and how after rebuilding it several times it was bombed again and again by Muslims. I related how Muslims kidnapped me to kill me, but that God saved me from their hands. I spoke about the horrors of the war and the atrocities committed by both Muslims and Christians.

If you were in the audience, would you have thought about anything the imam said? I was talking about real issues of life and death, generated by hate. But my theme was love.

The stage was set for me to speak about the love that overwhelmed me and transformed my life, taking away all the hatred from my heart. While I was giving my testimony, you could have heard the smallest pin drop. Everyone was curious about where I was going with this. "I love each one of you and

---

[5] I John 3:18.

want to share with you the greatest news you could ever hear." I stressed that Jesus came to give us life by rescuing us from sin, Satan, and death. "He did not come to earth to establish a religion, but a relationship."

I went on to speak about his great forgiveness. I was straightforward with them when I explained that what I was about to tell them would be difficult for them to swallow from a human standpoint. God becoming a man is inconceivable to our human mind. Yet if it is the truth, it is an awesome truth. "Just because you do not understand God, does it mean you reject his offer of salvation?" I used my full forty five minutes to explain God's cosmic plan of salvation, demonstrating that through Jesus there is forgiveness of sin, true peace with God, and eternal life. Of course, my message of love did not satisfy everyone. Jesus had already warned that many will hate us.

During the question-and-answer time there were many negative comments and challenging questions. Because I have done this a number of times, I was prepared for what was to come next: some trouble-makers wanted to provoke me. They pointed out that I did not answer the imam and that I should have done so. I told them that we had an entire hour to answer their questions. When a really tough question was thrown at me I was determined to handle it with all the love I could muster. I responded gently and with respect. [6] I tried to help them understand, not to prove them or their imam wrong. In situations like this, sometimes it is best not to fully answer every question. Often there is no right answer to a wrong question. Sometimes the best answer is another question that gets someone to think. Isn't that what Jesus did?

After two-and-a-half hours of this exchange with hundreds of Muslims from many Arab nations, the imam faded away and hardly opened his mouth afterward. I did not use this opportunity to show them how bad Islam is, how evil

---

[6] I Peter 3:15.

Muhammad was, or how false the Qur'an is. Rather, I used this unique opportunity to share the love of Christ, not only in direct words such as, "Jesus loves you," but more importantly, through my attitude. My manner of speaking was just as important as the actual words that I said. The InterVarsity leader who invited me for the debate commented, "At least no one went away thinking you hate them."

Guess what happened next? The official debate was over, the imam and I shook hands, and he headed home. As for me, I was surrounded by dozens of Arabs who wanted to speak in Arabic (the debate itself was in English). They asked me questions. I sought the guidance of the God's Spirit to answer them as clearly and lovingly as I could. That lasted for several hours. People are drawn by love and repulsed by hate. I operated by the principle that Paul articulated: "Do not let any unwholesome talk come out of your mouths, but only what is helpful for building others up according to their needs, that it may benefit those who listen." [7]

No one loves as Jesus did. His great love cost him much suffering and pain, and ultimately his temporal life. He loved everyone and had compassion toward all, including those he offended.

Of course, no Christian worker would admit that his or her methods are not loving. We all claim that our approach is true love. The fact is that love has many facets and different expressions. What is important is whether or not the audience saw my action as loving. I am sure some saw it as weakness, but hopefully some perceived the strength of love. But I would rather risk being seen as weak and loving than strong and

---

[7] Ephesians 4:29.

hateful. I told the truth in love, I stuck to the issues, did not return evil for evil, and blessed them instead of cursing them. [8]

The Power of Love

Cubs to Lions is Horizons International's discipleship and training program for Christians from Muslim Backgrounds (CMBs). In May 2010, men and women from various Muslim backgrounds attended the annual week-long event. Many of them were new believers, as recent as two months old in the faith. Their hunger and thirst for spiritual reality was amazing. I began teaching them the basics of the Bible, and within two hours it was apparent that the Spirit of God was working in a new way for some of them. As I spoke about the love of the glorious God who came down to save us, one CMB from Iran stood up with a beaming smile and said, "WOW! This is amazing, this is amazing! God comes down to us and even dies for us? This is amazing!" Her fresh exuberance was contagious, and we all reveled in God's glory as others in the room began having similar moments of discovery. This really is the heart of the Gospel. Jesus said, "God demonstrates his own love for us in this: while we were still sinners, Christ died for us." [9]

The love of God has the power to transform lives. But most Muslims are not aware of what this Iranian girl discovered that day: that the Good News is this "amazing." I am convinced that the only way they can understand the love of God

---

[8] "I came to you in weakness and fear, and with much trembling," (I Corinthians 2:3); "Instead, speaking the truth in love, we will in all things grow up into him who is the Head, that is, Christ," (Ephesians 4:15); "Be not overcome of evil, but overcome evil with good," (Romans 12:21); "Bless those who curse you, pray for those who mistreat you," (Luke 6:28).

[9] Romans 5:8.

is through the love that they can see, touch, and feel that flows from us to them in practical ways. John the disciple expressed it clearly this way, "For anyone who does not love his brother, whom he has seen, cannot love God, whom he has not seen."[10] Though this refers to loving others the way we love God, the reverse is also true, that people often cannot understand the love of God, whom they cannot see, unless they see the love of his children.

Love in Action

The war in Kosova in 1999 drove one million Albanians to the neighboring countries. The nation was devastated. Most stores were broken into and looted. Many buildings were destroyed. The church was small. Perhaps there were no more than one hundred known Christians from Muslim backgrounds among the 2.2 million Muslims.

As I went to see what Horizons International could do to help, we decided that it would be best to let the church, no matter how small it was, begin to serve the needy people. After much discussion and prayer we agreed to form a church-run, national humanitarian organization to coordinate the efforts of several foreign aid organizations in meeting the needs of the returning refugees after the war ended.

Based on the passage from 1 Thessalonians 1:3, we found no better name than *Aksioni i Dashuris,* which means "Love in Action." It was also a very appropriate name because the acronym was "AID." That is what we were trying to do, aid the refugees to get back on their feet. Tens of thousands were served by this ministry thanks to generous donors and the help of some of the mission agencies that participated. This ministry was led by Albanians from the various young churches in Kosova. This was the love of Christ as it is sup-

---

[10] 1 John 4:20.

posed to function. Through God's people, in the real world, playing an important role in a time of need.

When you describe nature as beautiful you are talking about its visible qualities, colors, shapes, textures and aromas. These are tangible qualities. But how about love? What does it look like? It is abstract and remains hidden in the heart of the lover until it finds practical expression. This is our challenge, to put our love into action in practical ways.

Chapter 15

An Open Door that No One Can Shut

It is no secret that reaching Muslims is one of the greatest challenges facing the Church of Jesus Christ in our century. Alas, the Church has not yet stepped up to and met this challenge. By and large, Christians everywhere are oblivious to God's mandate to reach out to the Muslim world. The Body of Christ needs to rise up and answer God's calling, living out its mission.

When Jesus called his disciples to follow him he did not mean it to be some romantic, gushy, sweet invitation. He was blunt, and made it absolutely clear that to follow him they must deny themselves, carry the cross, and lose their lives. [1] Jesus had just told them, "I will build my Church." In effect, Jesus was saying, "I will build my Church, and I want to use *you*, but it will cost you *everything*. You must leave everything behind, including your own life. Follow me, and I will train you to be fishers of men."

Twelve ordinary men accomplished the extraordinary and turned the world upside down. The Jewish rulers of the time recognized the power inside the disciples and they were amazed. "When they saw the courage of Peter and John and realized that they were unschooled, ordinary men, they were astonished and they took note that these men had been with Jesus." [2]

This call to action was not restricted to the disciples of his day. It is also our calling today. We need to take it personally,

---

[1] Luke 9:23, Matthew 16:18.

[2] Acts 4:13.

and apply everything that Jesus taught his disciples to our own lives.

Open Your Eyes and Look at the Fields![3] The Harvest is Plentiful, but the Workers are Few[4]

In training his disciples, Jesus wanted them to see the world through his eyes. He modeled for them how he thought and felt about people. Many times in the gospels we read that Jesus asked his disciples to open their eyes. He wanted them to see the immensity of the harvest, that the harvest is ripe, and to give them a heart of compassion toward the people.

Since I was in elementary school in the 1950s, the global Muslim population has grown at a staggering rate. Today, there are an estimated 1.2 billion Muslims worldwide, and there are no signs of that growth slowing in the foreseeable future. Are our evangelistic efforts even keeping up with the birth rate? In my view we are barely scratching the surface. Missionaries to the fifty-six Muslim majority nations are scarce, numbering in the dozens–or at most in the hundreds–in certain countries. In most of these nations the Church is small and poor. For a breakthrough to occur, we must open our eyes and see that the harvest is plentiful and that the laborers are still few. Then we must do something about it: *we* must be those laborers.

The Harvest is Ripe[5]

Just two decades ago, Muslims had little exposure to Christianity. Even in countries where Christians were present, there was little interaction with them. But the information

---

[3] John 4:35.

[4] Matthew 9:35-38.

[5] John 4:35.

age has given Muslims and Christians access to each other in ways that were unimaginable before. Globalization and the massive shuffling of peoples between continents are exposing Muslims to Christianity. Immigrating refugees and asylum seekers, international students and scholars, businessmen, and many other visitors to the USA are coming into contact with Christians on a daily basis. The world is shrinking. Which major city in the world does not have people from every nation, language, and tribe? In Los Angeles at least 224 languages are spoken at home, and 92 of them in the Los Angeles School District. [6]

American cities are not the only ones with such multicultural diversity. Go to any major city or university town in the world–Tokyo, Singapore, Cairo, Istanbul, Cape Town, Mumbai, or Dubai–and you will find the world in microcosm.

Satellite TV and the Internet are giving Muslims the opportunity to investigate Christianity in phenomenal numbers. One Christian website alone had over 100 million visitors in one year, and there are hundreds of similar websites. As I visit Muslim countries and interact with Muslims, I find that most of my contacts have visited Christian sites. I have found them to be like ripe fruit, waiting to be picked. God promised that his word will not return in vain, [7] that it will always accomplish God's purposes. We have to believe that at least some of the millions who are watching Christian programs in their own languages are ripe for the harvest. As Jesus told his disciples, "Do you not say, 'Four months more and then the harvest'? I tell you, open your eyes and look at the fields! They are ripe for harvest." [8]

---

[6] According to a study by Professor Vyacheslav Ivanov of UCLA.

[7] Isaiah 55:10,11.

[8] John 4:35.

Jesus Wept [9]

I looked down from the balcony of a tall building in the center square of Latakia, Syria. Massive crowds crisscrossed in all directions. Cars, bicycles, donkeys, dogs, and people were all whisking by each other and swarming like ants. I had come there with an Operation Mobilization team in 1969. The task of reaching the city with our small OM team suddenly became overwhelming. I imagined Jesus standing next to me and feeling moved. I recalled that when Jesus saw the crowds, his heart was stirred with compassion. When he looked over to Jerusalem from the Mount of Olives, he cried. [10] When he stood by the tomb of Lazarus, he wept. I was sure Jesus would cry over the masses in Latakia, and every other Muslim city. I couldn't hold back my own tears.

If our hearts are not moved by the depravity and lostness of Muslims, we will never be able to reach them effectively. It is our love that compels us, our compassion that drives us, and our conviction that they *are* headed to hell without Christ that propels us to action.

When I was black-listed from Iraq in 1979 because of my work in Kurdistan, I allowed discouragement to harden my heart. It had taken six years of hardships and dangers to finish the Sorani New Testament. Then it seemed that it was all in vain. I lost my passion and my heart grew cold toward the Kurds. I did not have the eyes of faith to see beyond my present predicament. Many years passed. The Gulf War broke out. Kurdistan became accessible for the first time. The closed door flung open. I pleaded with God to give me tears for the Kurds again. It was a painful, daily wait on my face for three months until God opened my tear ducts.

---

[9] John 11:35.

[10] Luke 19:41.

Battling with God for souls is painful, but battle for souls we must. Jesus modeled it for us for forty days in the desert. When was the last time you cried for the lostness of people who do not know Christ? Allow your heart to be broken with what breaks God's heart.

See, I Have Placed Before You an Open Door that No One Can Shut [11]

The Iron Curtain in the communist era did not stop Brother Andrew. He penetrated the "closed doors" with the power of the Gospel. He became known as God's smuggler for taking the word of God behind the Iron Curtain in large numbers. What was his secret? Everyone was calling the Soviet Union a "closed door." Brother Andrew did not see it that way, and that is why he named his mission "Open Doors." When Brother Andrew came to my college to tell his stories in 1969, I asked the Lord, "Please Lord, help me see the cracks in the walls of Islam."

Kosova was not on my radar screen. I knew little about Eastern Europe. When I heard in 1994 that missionary work among the Albanian Muslims of Kosova was almost nonexistent, I sensed God's call to go. But the doors seemed totally closed. The Yugoslav Embassy denied my visa application, and when I called to inquire, the man at the office swore at me and hung up. The Serbs were mad at the USA and they were turning Americans away. The handful of new believers in the country tried to get me a visa from the inside. That was also denied. Still, as I prayed about it, I felt strongly that I needed to go. So I flew to Bulgaria anyway, reasoning that, "If God called me to come here, he will make a way where there is no way." Once I arrived, I took the bus through Macedonia, where I heard a rumor that some Americans had been humili-

---

[11] Revelation 3:8.

ated at the border by being stripped, robbed, and turned back on foot. I really started questioning the wisdom of my decision, when suddenly my mind went to the cross where Jesus hung, stripped and naked. Paul's words in Philippians 3:10 gained a fresh, new meaning for me: "I want to know Christ and the power of his resurrection and the fellowship of sharing in his sufferings, becoming like him in his death, and so, somehow, to attain to the resurrection from the dead." [12] Indeed, it is a privilege to share in the suffering of our savior, and God used this to encourage me to keep moving forward. The last couple miles before the border were bumper-to-bumper, with engines shut-off. I grabbed my bag, got off the bus, and made my way through the rows of cars. I was turned away at the first guard station, so I went to the next. All six threw my passport back once they saw the eagle on the front. Still not ready to give up, I found a bench to sit on for a while, to figure out what to do. After a half-hour, my hope crept back as I noticed a new crew of border officers had arrived to relieve the previous shift. Ten minutes later I mustered my faith and tried all six booths again. "Prishtina, Prishtina!" I urged them, motioning toward the capital city. None of them spoke English, and I didn't speak Serbian or Albanian, so my attempts to communicate were futile.

That's when I really got frustrated. Doubt, discouragement, and self-condemning words crept into my head: "You are a fool to waste all this money and time to come all the way here without a visa. Everyone told you they wouldn't let you in. Why didn't you listen?" I sat there on the bench with my head between my knees and cried out to God. "Lord did you bring me here or did I come by my own volition? God, did you call me to Kosova, or am I forcing your hand? Father, your will be done, not mine. Master, what about the 2.2 million Albanian Muslims who have not yet heard the Gospel?"

---

[12] Philippians 3:10,11.

I looked up to see two officers coming straight toward me. Grabbing me by the arms, they led me toward the station. "Here it comes," I thought. They took me to the Chief of Police, who spoke a bit of English.

"Why you want go to Prishtina?"

I told him that my goal was to preach about Jesus to the Muslim Albanians.

He paused, looked at me, and said, "This good. Welcome to Serbia." He stamped my passport himself, and shook my hand. It turns out he was Serbian Orthodox, and would be happy if I succeeded. I stepped out of the building on the other side of the border just in time to see my bus pull out, finally having made it through the traffic!

That trip turned out to be pivotal for the work of God in Kosova (which was then a province of Serbia). Horizons International has been deeply involved in Kosova since that first visit. On October 16, 1994, the Messiah Evangelical Church was organized, with six believers. Since that time, Femi, the pastor, kept strict records of every person who came in and out, those who remained faithful and those who slid back. By the time the war broke out in March 1999, there were fifty-eight believers. It took hard work and a determined emphasis on discipleship through grounding the believers in the word to get to this stage in five years. During that time I took three or four trips to Kosova every year, giving them intensive teaching, encouragement, and evangelism training. In 1999, we saw the war coming, so I went to prepare them spiritually for it.

My main focus in the months leading up to the war was preparing them for the challenges ahead. From my experience in Kurdistan, the war was going to bring numerous humanitarian agencies into the country. Some of these were Christian groups. I knew that the young church, with almost no exposure to the rest of the world, was going to go through a period of trials that could make or break it. The lessons learned will have to wait for a book on church planting. But for now I want to stress how God, in his sovereignty, protected the church from near destruction. Some key leaders in the church fell away. Most of the believers became refugees in neighboring countries. The church was scattered and its future was unclear. But the church survived, thanks to the faithfulness of a few brothers and sisters under the wise leadership of Femi Cakolli.

On July 1, 1999, my daughter, Noelle, and I escorted twenty-three exiled believers back to Kosova in three vans. We had driven through Albania and Macedonia looking for the believers in refugee camps. Devastation and destruction was everywhere. Noelle, who was a theater student at the time, interviewed and recorded numerous testimonies of the believers telling their war stories. The result was *Wings of Refuge,* a one-woman performance relating the stories of these men and women and how they saw the hand of God in their lives. Amazingly, Psalm 91 was used by God to encourage and sustain almost all of those interviewed. At that time, the church in Kosova was about to experience significant growth and expansion. Many fell away, but the church goes on.

On the tenth anniversary of the church, Oct 16, 2004, hundreds of believers crammed into a large theater to celebrate God's faithfulness. Pastors, elders, and members of some thirty churches were represented. In my keynote address, I related the story of God's faithfulness, from that day on the border in June 1994 until the present. There was much rejoicing. That day when the doors seemed to be closed, I could not have even dreamed that ten years later I would celebrate with pastors who at the time were Muslims struggling to survive the aftermath of communism. As an added bonus, a highly competent music group made up of young, zealous and promising young people played various instruments.

In October 2009, fifteen years after my first visit, thirty-five pastors gathered at a conference center to receive our *Engaging Islam* training. They wanted to see the Church grow beyond the few thousand who have come to know Christ in the last fifteen years, all from a Muslim background.

In no way do I take credit for all of this. Many mission agencies came in and participated both in the recovery of the country and the growth of the church. As I pointed out at a conference for all agencies involved in Kosova, echoing the sentiment of the great Apostle Paul, "I planted the seed, Apollos watered it, but God made it grow. So neither he who plants nor he who waters is anything, but only God, who makes things grow." [13] To him, and him alone, be all glory and praise, now and evermore.

Nothing is too hard for God. He makes a way where there seems to be no way, and opens doors that no one can shut.

When God calls you, he will open the doors for you, even though they may seem shut. Whether it is a border, a visa, enough money for your support, or opportunities to witness; open your eyes of faith and see that the door is wide open.

Feed My Sheep [14]

The Muslim world is our responsibility. The Church, and each member of it, is entrusted with the Great Commission. In his training program, Jesus seemed to deliberately overwhelm his disciples with the burden of the harvest.

After being extremely tired one day because of the huge crowds, Jesus promised them rest. [15] They got into their boat and began to look for a "solitary place." As soon as they stepped on the shore, more than five thousand gathered around them, from every village and town around the lake. Mark adds these words: "And Jesus taught them many things." The disciples must have been murmuring to each other, "When will he finish teaching them?" They waited and waited. Finally they were hungry, and could not wait anymore. "Send

---

[13] I Corinthians 3:6-7.

[14] John 21:15-18.

[15] Mark 6:31.

the people away," they said. Then came the shocking instruction, "You give them something to eat." He wanted *them* to take responsibility. They had work to do. He expected them to do it.

Was Jesus joking when he told twelve men to feed over five thousand people? Did he have no consideration for the sheer logistics of feeding all these people? Certainly, he did not think of the cost! This story shows that the disciples still did not have a heart for the people. The disciples saw the task as a chore, as a distraction, as an inconvenience, as an exorbitant expense.

Are we any different? How do we see the massive immigration of Muslims to our neighborhoods? Is it an invasion, an intrusion? Or is it an opportunity that God is bringing to our doorsteps, that we may see, open our hearts, and act?

One of the most amazing lessons in this story is that Jesus, who could turn stones into bread, asked his disciples to give him what *they* had. He wanted to demonstrate that when we do whatever we can do, he will do what he alone can do. When we give him what we have, he will give us what he has. When we are faithful in the little, he will give us the increase.

This story alone should be enough to get us to forget about all the barriers and roadblocks we face as we reach the masses. God is looking for hearts that feel the agony, the pain, the lostness and depravity of man. Only then–only when we feel it deep in our hearts–will we see the miracle. Try it.

Paul recognized that his calling came out of the grace of God, who wants to give us a role, a share in the blessings and the glory: "I do all this for the sake of the gospel, that I may share in its blessings." [16] "He called you to this through our gospel, that you might share in the glory of our Lord Jesus Christ." [17]

---

[16] 1 Corinthians 9:23.

[17] 2 Thessalonians 2:14.

Do you want to share in the blessings, in God's glory? Then open your eyes and see. Open your heart and feel. Open your pocket and give. Open your mouth and speak!

Opportunities Abound

Muslims are spread across the globe in a great diaspora. With millions of Muslims throughout the nations, they are within reach. You can find them on university campuses, airports, parks, and shopping malls. Many of you could have a Muslim in your neighborhood. If not, you can go the extra mile and find them. If you have an internet connection, you can befriend a Muslim. [18]

Countries which have been typically closed to the Gospel witness, like Saudi Arabia, are now sending thousands of students to live on our campuses and in our neighborhoods. Sadly, the great majority of them never step into a Christian's home.

Satan would like us to believe that Muslims are unreachable in order to discourage us and instill a spirit of defeat into God's children. Until we have given Muslims the opportunity to hear the Gospel we cannot say that Muslims are resistant. Thousands of Muslims have come to Christ in the last decade alone, in response to preaching, teaching, radio, correspondence courses, and Bible distribution. The Internet has penetrated thick walls that two decades ago were thought impenetrable. Christians from Muslim Backgrounds are popping up everywhere; in fact, they are taking the lead in many new ministries. The growth is exponential, and CMBs are becoming such a significant minority that, in some countries, governments are beginning to officially recognize their status as Christians. Once I stood on the balcony of a conference hall and looked down on a gathering for CMBs. What did I see? A

---

[18] Facebook, Paltalk, and Skype are three easy ways to make Muslim friends.

beautiful tapestry of men and women, children and adults from all walks of life from around the globe, worshipping Jesus together. The zeal of those who have left Islam and have come to Christ puts all of us to shame. Is God making us jealous of them?

My challenge to the Church everywhere, and to every Christian, is to step out of the comfort zone, defy the norm, and make the world its priority, Muslims included.

Jesus Christ came down from heaven to engage humanity. Now he's calling us to engage our world. Engaging Islam begins when you engage one Muslim.

About the Author

Born and raised in Lebanon, Georges Houssney's background in psychology, linguistics, and intercultural studies has contributed to the production of two books in Arabic, Bible translation projects in Arabic and Kurdish, an indigenous Arabic Bible study curriculum in cooperation with David. C. Cook Foundation, and the thirteen-year publication of *ReachOut to the Muslim World*.

His travels to ninety-eight countries and his forty years of experience in evangelism, discipleship, and church planting have culminated in the development of two training programs: *Engaging Islam*, for church members and missionaries, and *Cubs to Lions*, for Christians from Muslim backgrounds. As founder and president of Horizons International, Georges, along with his family and global staff members, strives to awaken the Church to the task of boldly proclaiming the Gospel to the nations.

To learn more about Georges' ministry, visit:
horizonsinternational.org

For information about training, visit:
engagingislam.org

For articles and discussion on biblical missions, visit:
biblicalmissiology.org

To inquire about Georges speaking at your church or event, send an email to: info@engagingislam.org